The secret to living with charm, grace, balance, and joie de vivre—it's all here in *Year of Tranquility*! **—Jamie Cat Callan, author of *Parisian Charm School***

If you're moving through a big life transition or simply seeking a bit more grace and joy in your days, *Year of Tranquility* is like having a wise and loving bestie right in your pocket—gently nudging you toward the best version of yourself and always cheering you on as you go. **—Flora Bowley, artist and author of *Brave Intuitive Painting* and *Creative Revolution***

Kimberly's new combination *Year of Tranquility* with a planner is a luscious buffet of marvelous self-care and empowerment topics and strategies that we are all striving to experience regularly and master! She begins with helping you to set SMART goals and then challenges you to commit to your intentions interwoven with exquisite moments of self-care indulgences, such as staying in bed all day, eating on your good china, making art journals, practicing meaningful meditations, joyful travel, and sharing your gifts with the world in a meaningful way that reflects your essence. This life guide has an abundance of clever and appealing prompts and ideas that will keep you in tune with making your journey into a compelling story of fulfillment and wonder. There is something here for everyone to muse and revel in! Indeed it is a tranquility treasure chest with years of potential inspirations and challenges to grow into as we evolve. I have used Kimberly's pink planners and have given them as gifts in the past. But this new comprehensive version is masterful and rich with invitations for a lifetime! Magnifique! **—Gail McMeekin, LICSW, creative success catalyst, author of *The 12 Secrets of Highly Creative Women* series, and *The Power of Positive Choices***

I want this book! I need this book! I've seen creativity journals before but never one so packed full of wisdom, practical, easy-to-implement tips, and so much style. I am going to buy *Year of Tranquility* as a gift not just for myself but for all my friends. **—Beth M. Howard, blogger at The World Needs More Pie.com and author of *Making Piece: A Memoir of Love, Loss and Pie***

Kimberly is the personification of elegance, grace, and chic. In her new book she shares her tranquility secrets in an easy to reference month by month playbook, filled with delightful tools guaranteed to nourish and inspire the dreamer who is ready to actualize their dreams. *Year of Tranquility* is a must have for all women, girls or boys of any age or gender. **—Sharon Gannon, Jivamukti Yoga**

In a world full of books about how to live a joyful life, *Year of Tranquility* stands out in the way Kimberly artfully brings together personal stories with practical advice. The book feels like an exquisitely wrapped box of chocolates, holding small but potent intentions, practices, and habits to sweep away the clutter, get clear on what is most important, and live a meaningful life. **—Christine Mason Miller, author and artist**

Year of Tranquility

A LIFESTYLE PLANNER

by Kimberly Wilson, LICSW, MA

Copyright 2019 by Kimberly Wilson

All rights reserved. This book may not be reproduced in whole or in part, stored in a retrieval system, or transmitted in any form or by any means—electronic, mechanical, or other—without written permission from the publisher, except by a reviewer, who may quote brief passages in a review.

DISCLAIMER: This publication contains the opinions and ideas of its author. The advice contained herein is for informational purposes only. Please consult your medical professional before beginning any diet or exercise program. Every effort has been made to ensure the information contained in this book is complete and accurate.

ISBN: 978-0-578-43803-0
Printed in the United States of America

Cover photo, pp. 7, 10, 13, 18, 22, 25, 30, 36, 38, 40, 48, 63, 91, 176, 229 by Marie Maroun
pp. 35, 163, 230, back cover by Tim Mooney
pp. 38, 217, 230 by Patrick Onofre
p. 230 Carla Coulson
All others by Kimberly Wilson
p. 137 Illustration by Mary Catherine Starr
Layout design by Christy Jenkins • seewhydesignworks.com

acknowledgements

MANY SPECIAL BEINGS HELPED MAKE THIS PROJECT POSSIBLE, INCLUDING:

Tim Mooney, who is my best friend, cheerleader, and right hand.

Mama, Linda Wilson, who showed up with bells on for the *Year of Tranquility* program and pointed out my typos along the way.

Pops, Steve Wilson, who inspired the writing craft and love of photography at an early age.

Rescues Mookie, Belle Starr, Gizmo, and Jackson Wilson Mooney, who make my heart flutter.

Designer Christy Jenkins, who beautifully brings my vision to life.

Beloved beta readers who generously offered their editing eyes to this project. Thank you, thank you, thank you!

Carol Meyers for her eagle eye and kind contributions.

Readers and listeners of *Tranquility du Jour*, thank you for giving me a home.

THIS BOOK IS DEDICATED
TO THOSE AROUND THE GLOBE
WHO SUPPORTED THE
TRANQUILITY DU JOUR DAYBOOK/PLAYBOOK
AND THE
YEAR OF TRANQUILITY
PROGRAM.

DEEP BOWS TO YOU!

Year of Tranquility

A LIFESTYLE PLANNER

TABLE OF CONTENTS

PART I: PLAN

INTRODUCTION	10
MANIFESTO	12
TRANQUILITY DU JOUR TENETS	13
TRANQUILITY TOOLS	15
SEASONAL LIFE REVIEW	21
YEAR'S DREAMS	22
YEAR'S LAYOUT	26
LISTS	28
TIME TRACKING	32
HEALTH	34
CAPSULE DRESSING	38
TRANQUIL TRAVEL	39
BUDGET	40
30 DAYS OF TRANQUILITY	43

PART II: PRACTICE

MONTHLY PAGES AND ESSAYS	44
DREAMS	48
LOVE	63
STYLE + BEAUTY	74
CREATIVITY	91
MINIMALISM	105
WELLNESS	119
YOGA	132
SELF-CARE	146
MINDFULNESS	163
WRITING	176
ENTREPRENEURSHIP	191
MEANING	206
TYING A BOW	217
YEAR'S REVIEW	218
A LETTER TO MY FUTURE SELF	220
INSPIRATION PAGES	221
LOVE NOTE	229
ABOUT KIMBERLY	230

introduction

"AND THE DAY CAME WHEN THE RISK TO REMAIN TIGHT IN A BUD WAS MORE PAINFUL THAN THE RISK IT TOOK TO BLOOM."
— ANAÏS NIN

Year of Tranquility *is the marriage of a big picture planner with 12 months of deep diving into a variety of topics designed to bring awareness into daily life.*

Filled with practices that are gentle nudges toward making choices that soothe rather than stress, my hope is that this book serves as a tool for self-discovery and meaning-making for the year ahead.

PLANNING YOUR YEAR

Start anytime and move through this year-long program at your own pace. Explore the various tools and lists in Part I. Note what piques your curiosity. Begin by completing a Seasonal Life Review (p. 21) and capturing your Year's Dreams (p. 22). To make it your own, there's ample space to reflect and dream with a gold pen in hand.

After the initial planning and lifestyle pieces, you'll find 12 essays followed by four suggested practices that align with the month's themes in Part II.

January: Dreams
February: Love
March: Style + Beauty
April: Creativity
May: Minimalism
June: Wellness

July: Yoga
August: Self-care
September: Mindfulness
October: Writing
November: Entrepreneurship
December: Meaning

MONTHLY

Each month pen your Month's Dreams (what you want to manifest) and Month's Review (how it unfolded), read and reflect on the monthly essay, create space for the complementary weekly practices, and consider the monthly Tranquility Tools (p. 17). Cheers to entertaining, volunteering, and reading two books!

WEEKLY

To stay connected to your intentions, set aside one hour each week to dabble in the suggested weekly practices following the month's essay, reflect on its impact, and engage in the weekly Tranquility Tools (p. 16). Let's clear clutter, pen a love note, and plan our MITs (Most Important Tasks).

DAILY

When possible, set up your days with restorative rituals such as journaling, AM and PM routines, and mindful movement. Review the daily Tranquility Tools (p. 15) for more inspiration. Take a few minutes each day to savor and exhale.

MAKE IT YOUR OWN

Or scrap the whole system and make it entirely your own. Pick it up when you crave an inspiration infusion. Doodle. Dive into the topics that you most need at the moment.

Year of Tranquility is filled with suggested practices from my two decades of entrepreneurial and mindfulness experience, blended with my study of positive psychology and journal therapy, and work as a psychotherapist and designer. Think of me as a gentle guide who is also on the journey with you.

Let's bloom into who we want to be and how we want to be. Pen your plans, explore new practices, and check the boxes (so fulfilling!). Personalize it with ephemera, colored markers, washi tape, and your deepest desires.

bisous,
Kimberly

 @TRANQUILITYDUJOUR

 @TRANQUILITYDUJOUR

 @TRANQUILITYDUJOUR

#YEAROFTRANQUILITY

KIMBERLYWILSON.COM

manifesto

I BELIEVE IN HANDWRITTEN NOTES. I BELIEVE IN USING CHINA AT EVERY MEAL. I BELIEVE IN THE HEALING POWER OF BUBBLE BATHS. I BELIEVE THAT YOU'RE NEVER TOO OLD TO WEAR A TUTU. I BELIEVE IN EQUALITY FOR ALL. I BELIEVE PARIS IS A DELIGHT TO ALL SENSES. I BELIEVE IN STARGAZING AND OBSERVING THE MOON'S PHASES. I BELIEVE THAT COMPASSION IS THE NEW BLACK. I BELIEVE IN LAZY SUNDAY MORNINGS. I BELIEVE THAT MAGIC HAPPENS ON THE YOGA MAT. I BELIEVE IN EATING PLANTS. I BELIEVE IN HIGH TEA AT ALL TIMES OF THE DAY. I BELIEVE IN LIVING LIFE FULL OUT. I BELIEVE NATURE HEALS. I BELIEVE THAT WRITING IS A TOOL FOR DISCOVERY. I BELIEVE WOMEN CAN CHANGE THE WORLD. I BELIEVE IN DONNING NOIR AND LIVING PINK. I BELIEVE THAT GLITTER AND WASHI TAPE SPARK JOY. I BELIEVE IN THE EASE OF A CAPSULE WARDROBE. I BELIEVE IN LIGHTING CANDLES EVERY DAY. I BELIEVE USING PAINT, COLLAGE, AND PENS TO AWAKEN OUR INNER ARTIST. I BELIEVE IN TWINKLE LIGHTS YEAR-ROUND. I BELIEVE IN SEEKING BALANCE BETWEEN DOING AND BEING. I BELIEVE WE HAVE A RESPONSIBILITY TO MAKE A DIFFERENCE. I BELIEVE IN HAPPINESS AND FREEDOM FOR ALL BEINGS.

tranquility du jour tenets

Tranquility du Jour *offers an online and in-person space to explore living fully and intentionally. Started as a blog in 2004, and then a podcast, we've grown into a sweet global community of like-hearted dreamers on a path to infuse more tranquility into our lives.*

Below are the five principles of living the *Tranquility du Jour* lifestyle.

1. **COMPASSION:** Through our daily choices, we strive to alleviate the suffering of all beings, including furry, scaled, and feathered ones. We treat others as we'd like to be treated. We honor the environment and do all we can to protect it through recycling and using only what we need. We help speak for those who don't have a voice.

2. **CREATIVITY:** We connect with our creative spark and let it shine through art, crafts, writing, setting a table with flair, or living out loud. Our surroundings reflect our creative style. We see most activities as a way to express our creativity and refuel our creative well regularly through reading, taking classes, and practicing. Our life is art.

3. **STYLE + BEAUTY:** How we present ourselves to the world and how we experience the world affect how we feel. We choose a signature style that is personal and reflects who we are. Our homes and offices are set up in a way that nurtures our spirits. Since what we put inside our bodies shows on the outside, we fuel ourselves with whole foods and occasional indulgences. We are moved by the arts, flowers, and simple pleasures.

4. **MINDFULNESS:** We bring awareness to how we spend our days. Through practices such as meditation and yoga, we connect with our minds and bodies. We intentionally choose how to spend our time, energy, and money to reflect our values. Practicing simplicity and seeking meaning guides us toward what matters most.

5. **SELF-CARE:** The act of nourishing ourselves is akin to breathing. Reflecting through journaling, setting morning and evening rituals, eating plants, and moving our bodies helps us stay in balance. We are lifelong learners and enjoy designing and following our dreams. We create meaningful community through healthy relationships, clear communication, and good boundaries.

TRANQUILITY IS THE QUALITY OF **CALM** WITHIN A **FULL AND MEANINGFUL** LIFE.

tranquility tools

**32 TOOLS TO ENHANCE YOUR
DAYS, WEEKS, MONTHS, AND SEASONS
WITH MEANINGFUL TRANQUILITY**

Tranquility Tools are daily, weekly, monthly, and seasonal practices to help align everyday activities with aspirations. Each is defined below. They serve as anchors to infuse the year with tranquility. These tools are listed throughout as reminders, along with a blank line for personalization.

8 DAILY TRANQUILITY TOOLS

1. **MORNING ROUTINE:** Greet your day with a yoga sun salutation, cuppa tea, or brisk walk with your beloved four-legged friend. Begin each morning with an intentional, tranquil tone.

2. **DAILY DRESS-UP:** Let your daily dress reflect your personality, lifestyle, and signature style. Add a dose of flair and don't forget your smile, good attitude, and vintage accessory.

3. **MINDFUL MOVEMENT:** Take a moment each day to move your body through dance, walking, or any other activity that makes your skin glisten. Bookend the experience with a dose of meditation by sitting still and connecting to your breath. Inhale, exhale, ommmm.

4. **EAT YOUR VEGGIES:** Reduce animal products and processed foods. Increase plant-based consumption for a joyful effect on your health, the planet, and animals.

5. **JOURNAL:** Spend a few moments penning your thoughts, noting highlights from your day, recurring dreams, what you consumed, how you're feeling, or anything else on your mind.

6. **GOAL REVIEW:** Read over your Month's Dreams each day. This helps those everyday decisions stay in alignment with your aspirations.

7. **GRATITUDE:** At the end of each day, note at least one thing for which you are grateful. It may be as simple as a warm bed or fresh water.

8. **EVENING ROUTINE:** End your day with reflection. Write in your journal, shut down your computer and smartphone, take a warm bath with Epsom salts, or read in bed for 30 minutes before lights out.

8 WEEKLY TRANQUILITY TOOLS

1. **PLAN WEEK'S MITS:** These are your most important tasks. Choose three to five projects to focus on each week and align your daily actions with bringing them to fruition. They are your week's road map.

2. **SOAK IN THE TUB:** This grounding practice helps clear the mind after a long day. Light candles, play music, or bring in a flute of your favorite libation. Allow yourself to melt into this sensual renewal practice.

3. **TAKE A DIGITAL DAY OFF:** Grant yourself a sabbatical from being glued to technology. Get your hands dirty in the garden, bake a pie, read a book, connect with a loved one, or collage in your art journal. Our connection to technology needs the off switch from time to time.

4. **CLEAR CLUTTER:** Piles of paperwork become mountains when not handled regularly. Take time each week to reduce the clutter around you. Watch yourself breathe easier and feel lighter.

5. **PEN A LOVE NOTE:** Reach out to a friend, family member, pen pal, or even yourself (a letter to your past or future self) with a thoughtful note. Let someone know you're thinking of

them and sending good thoughts. Insert a bag of tea, article of interest, or token of love. This sweet gesture goes a long way in our fast-paced society.

6. **BUY OR PICK FRESH FLOWERS:** Surround yourself with a pop of living color through potted plants, cut flowers, herbs, or bamboo stalks. If you have a garden, pick flowers and bring them into your living space to spruce up a barren bedside table.

7. **TAKE AN ARTIST DATE:** Julia Cameron, author of *The Artist's Way*, encourages a solo excursion to nurture your inner artist for one hour each week. Try a trip to a flower market, café, museum, bookstore, or art gallery and watch your ideas flourish.

8. **SAVOR A GREEN JUICE:** Infuse your body with healing nutrients found in a green juice. Watch your energy and vitality soar as you get a "direct shot of vitamins, minerals, enzymes, protein, and oxygen" per Kris Carr, author of *Crazy Sexy Diet*.

8 MONTHLY TRANQUILITY TOOLS

1. **CRAFT MONTH'S DREAMS:** At the start of each month, write your big dreams for the month. At the end of the month, review your list to give yourself a pat on the back for the items you accomplished, and carry over the ones that remain and still feel close to your heart.

2. **MANI/PEDI:** Nurture your nails by adding color, trimming your cuticles, and savoring an exfoliating footbath. Or, indulge in another form of well-deserved self-care.

3. **VOLUNTEER:** Give of your resources—time, money, or energy—to a favorite cause and watch how you can have a ripple effect on others and your own well-being.

4. **ENTERTAIN:** Invite a friend over for tea or host an intimate dinner fête. Don an apron, set the table, light candles, and channel your inner Martha Stewart.

5. **REVIEW YOUR BUDGET:** Spend less than you make, save a little, and donate, too. Set up a system for regular review. It doesn't have to be fancy; pen and paper with a pile of receipts work. Try the monthly budget review and the weekly spending chart (pp. 40–41). Or, go high tech with mint.com.

6. **READ TWO BOOKS:** To continually learn, grow, and expand your horizons, read and finish two books monthly. Watch your awareness grow.

7. **CREATE:** Bring something new into existence. Think intangible such as an idea or physical such as origami. Knit a scarf, make a banner, craft a meal, write blog posts, sew a dress, or paint a watercolor postcard.

8. **MASSAGE:** Massage has many benefits and is the perfect antidote to stressed, achy muscles. If a spa isn't in the cards, consider a neck or foot rub at your neighborhood nail salon, or check out the local massage school for good deals from therapists-in-training. Or, ask your beloved for a complimentary rub down.

8 SEASONAL TRANQUILITY TOOLS

1. **DO THE WHEEL OF LIFE:** Seasonally reflect on areas of your life such as work, style, creativity, dreams, home, self-care, spirituality, health, relationships, finances, etc. Rate each one with your level of satisfaction (10=bliss, 5=so-so, 0=boo). Review the areas that ranked lower than you'd like and pen three action steps to increase your satisfaction in them (p. 21).

2. **DEEP CLEAN:** Pull everything out of drawers, cupboards, closets, nooks, and crannies. Donate what no longer serves you, dust off what does, rotate seasonal wear, and put things back in their place with a renewed sense of order.

3. **PRACTICE ESSENTIALISM:** Review your life, personal and professional. Are you excited by what you see? Do plans

make you feel drained? Have you signed up for that one thing too many? What small shifts can you make to bring your day back into balance? Surrender the glorification of busy. Carve out time to savor.

4. **TAKE A BED DAY:** Create a few hours to an entire day for a rejuvenating day in bed. Gather your tools: candles, eye pillow, tea, water, books, journal, rose water spray, comfy clothes, soft linens, a chunky knit blanket. Anything that soothes. Begin with a luxurious soak in the tub. Add a splash of sweet almond oil and a few drops of lavender oil. Then saunter into your quiet space to rest and reset.

5. **TRY SOMETHING NEW:** Take up a new hobby, make vegan cheese, study a new language, pick up the guitar, join a writing group, take a modern dance class. Studies show that lifelong learning is directly tied to health and longevity.

6. **TEND YOUR GARDEN:** Seasonally it's good to pull weeds, repot plants, rake leaves, plant bulbs, and trim trees, even if you don't have a garden. Metaphorically, what would you like to plant, trim, repot, and clean up in your life? Observe what needs tending and do so with care.

7. **REARRANGE:** An important principle of Feng Shui (a Chinese philosophical system of harmonizing the environment) is that if you're feeling stuck, do some rearranging. Switch furniture, books, lamps, or art to create a fresh feeling in your surroundings.

8. **GET CULTURED:** Travel, head out for live music, watch your nearest ballet ensemble, read the classics (hello Jane Austen), get to know the Impressionists, try new-to-you cuisine, watch a Broadway musical, check out an exhibit, listen to classical music, or visit a winery or tea salon for a tasting.

A BED DAY IS BALM FOR THE SOUL.

seasonal life review

DATE: _____

SEASONALLY REFLECT ON AREAS OF YOUR LIFE. RATE EACH ONE WITH YOUR LEVEL OF SATISFACTION 10 = BLISS, 5 = SO-SO, 0 = BOO.

Here are some additional areas to consider: social life, romance, family, education, health, fitness, meaning, activism. Next, take a moment to note the areas that ranked low and create three action steps to increase your tranquility in these areas. Be gentle. Plant seeds. Watch dreams take root.

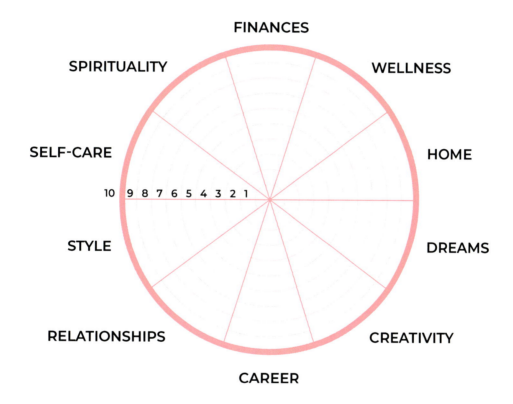

ACTION STEPS TO INCREASE AREAS THAT ARE LOWER THAN I'D LIKE:

year's dreams

DOODLE, LIST, COLLAGE, OR WRITE
WHAT YOU'D LIKE TO MANIFEST THIS YEAR.

MY WORD/THEME OF THE YEAR IS:

YEAR'S DREAMS

YEAR'S DREAMS

year's layout

JANUARY

FEBRUARY

MARCH

APRIL

MAY

JUNE

DOODLE, LIST, COLLAGE, OR WRITE DATES TO REMEMBER SUCH AS BIRTHDAYS, PLANS, IDEAS, EVENTS, OR ANYTHING ELSE OF NOTE FOR YOUR YEAR.

JULY

AUGUST

SEPTEMBER

OCTOBER

NOVEMBER

DECEMBER

24 BOOKS TO READ THIS YEAR

1. _____
2. _____
3. _____
4. _____
5. _____
6. _____
7. _____
8. _____
9. _____
10. _____
11. _____
12. _____
13. _____
14. _____
15. _____
16. _____
17. _____
18. _____
19. _____
20. _____
21. _____
22. _____
23. _____
24. _____

10 PLACES TO VISIT THIS YEAR

1. _____
2. _____
3. _____
4. _____
5. _____
6. _____
7. _____
8. _____
9. _____
10. _____

30 THINGS TO EXPERIENCE THIS YEAR

1. _____
2. _____
3. _____
4. _____
5. _____
6. _____
7. _____
8. _____
9. _____
10. _____
11. _____
12. _____
13. _____
14. _____
15. _____
16. _____
17. _____
18. _____
19. _____
20. _____
21. _____
22. _____
23. _____
24. _____
25. _____
26. _____
27. _____
28. _____
29. _____
30. _____

STOP + START LIST

WHAT I WANT MORE OF AND LESS OF THIS YEAR.

START

1. _____
2. _____
3. _____
4. _____
5. _____
6. _____
7. _____
8. _____
9. _____
10. _____
11. _____
12. _____
13. _____
14. _____
15. _____

STOP

1. _____
2. _____
3. _____
4. _____
5. _____
6. _____
7. _____
8. _____
9. _____
10. _____
11. _____
12. _____
13. _____
14. _____
15. _____

GRATITUDE

ONE THING I'M GRATEFUL FOR EACH WEEK.

1. _____
2. _____
3. _____
4. _____
5. _____
6. _____
7. _____
8. _____
9. _____
10. _____
11. _____
12. _____
13. _____
14. _____
15. _____
16. _____
17. _____
18. _____
19. _____
20. _____
21. _____
22. _____
23. _____
24. _____
25. _____
26. _____
27. _____
28. _____
29. _____
30. _____
31. _____
32. _____
33. _____
34. _____
35. _____
36. _____
37. _____
38. _____
39. _____
40. _____
41. _____
42. _____
43. _____
44. _____
45. _____
46. _____
47. _____
48. _____
49. _____
50. _____
51. _____
52. _____

current weekly schedule

TRACK HOW YOU CURRENTLY SPEND YOUR 168 HOURS:

	SUNDAY	MONDAY	TUESDAY	WEDNESDAY	THURSDAY	FRIDAY	SATURDAY
5 AM							
5:30							
6:00							
6:30							
7:00							
7:30							
8:00							
8:30							
9:00							
9:30							
10:00							
10:30							
11:00							
11:30							
12:00 PM							
12:30							
1:00							
1:30							
2:00							
2:30							
3:00							
3:30							
4:00							
4:30							
5:00							
5:30							
6:00							
6:30							
7:00							
7:30							
8:00							
8:30							
9:00							
9:30							
10:00							
10:30							
11:00							
11:30							
12:00 AM							

COMPARE YOUR TWO SCHEDULES AND LIST WAYS TO BRING PIECES OF THE IDEAL SCHEDULE INTO YOUR CURRENT ONE:

ideal weekly schedule

NOTE HOW YOU'D LIKE TO SPEND YOUR 168 HOURS:

Tune into *Tranquility du Jour* podcasts #199, #263, #306, and #343 where I discuss optimizing our days with *168 Hours* author Laura Vanderkam.

	SUNDAY	MONDAY	TUESDAY	WEDNESDAY	THURSDAY	FRIDAY	SATURDAY
5 AM							
5:30							
6:00							
6:30							
7:00							
7:30							
8:00							
8:30							
9:00							
9:30							
10:00							
10:30							
11:00							
11:30							
12:00 PM							
12:30							
1:00							
1:30							
2:00							
2:30							
3:00							
3:30							
4:00							
4:30							
5:00							
5:30							
6:00							
6:30							
7:00							
7:30							
8:00							
8:30							
9:00							
9:30							
10:00							
10:30							
11:00							
11:30							
12:00 AM							

TIME TRACKING

wellness planning

	SUNDAY	MONDAY	TUESDAY	WEDNESDAY	THURSDAY	FRIDAY	SATURDAY
BREAKFAST							
LUNCH							
DINNER							
WATER	○○○○ ○○○○	○○○○ ○○○○	○○○○ ○○○○	○○○○ ○○○○	○○○○ ○○○○	○○○○ ○○○○	○○○○ ○○○○
EXERCISE							
SLEEP							
MOOD							

SHOPPING LIST

○ _____
○ _____
○ _____
○ _____
○ _____
○ _____
○ _____
○ _____
○ _____
○ _____

○ _____
○ _____
○ _____
○ _____
○ _____
○ _____
○ _____
○ _____
○ _____
○ _____

PLANT-BASED PROTEINS

1. **NUTS:** walnuts, almonds, cashews, peanuts
2. **SEEDS:** flax, chia, pumpkin
3. **BEANS:** black, lima, kidney, chickpeas, lentils, edamame
4. **LEAFY GREENS:** spinach, kale, collards
5. **VEGGIES:** broccoli, peas, cauliflower, asparagus, corn
6. **OTHER:** quinoa, tofu, tempeh, and more!

meatless monday

I'm animal obsessed and on a mission to live my favorite mantra, *Lokah Samastah Sukhino Bhavantu*. Translated by yoga teacher Sharon Gannon as, "May all beings everywhere be happy and free. May the thoughts words and actions of my own life contribute in some way to that happiness and to that freedom for all." Ommmm. What a beautiful life message!

Going meatless, even once a week, lessens the risk of chronic conditions such as cancer, cardiovascular disease, diabetes, and obesity. It also reduces our carbon footprint and saves 28 land animals and 175 aquatic animals per year. Oh, and saves money, too!

Yes, by just one day a week. Good for us, the animals, and the environment! Tune into *Tranquility du Jour* podcasts #111, #186, #236, #303, #335, #349, #354, #365, #377, #391, #394. Learn more at kimberlywilson.com/animals.

MINDFUL EATING TIPS

1. Make eating an experience: light candles, set the table, and sit down.
2. Pack your plate with colorful plants, chew slowly, and savor each bite.
3. When eating, single task and only eat. Try dining in silence, sans TV, phone, or other distractions.
4. Pause between bites, put your fork down, and notice sensations. Read more about this in Self-Care.

detox

Feeling lethargic, overindulgent, or in need of a reset? Try this 7-day cleanse by combining self-care with clean food to release toxins, feel lighter, and rejuvenate.

BASIC PLAN

		DAY 1	DAY 2	DAY 3	DAY 4	DAY 5	DAY 6	DAY 7
A.M.	8OZ WARM WATER WITH LEMON AND 1-2 T GROUND FLAXSEED							
	GREEN SMOOTHIE OR CHIA SEED PUDDING							
	TONGUE SCRAPE							
	DRY SKIN BRUSH							
LUNCH	LUNCH MEAL*							
	EXERCISE							
P.M.	DINNER MEAL*							
	JOURNAL							
	BATH							
	HERBAL TEA							
	EXERCISE							

*MEAL IDEAS FOR LUNCH AND DINNER MIGHT INCLUDE MIXED GREENS SALAD, STEAMED VEGGIES OVER BROWN RICE, VEGGIE SOUP, SWEET POTATO NOODLES, SPICY HUMMUS, STUFFED AVOCADO OR RED PEPPER, LETTUCE WRAP BLACK BEAN TACOS, OR ROASTED VEGGIES WITH QUINOA.

INCLUDE

- Veggies (lots of dark leafy greens)
- Quinoa, brown rice, millet
- Beans, legumes, lentils
- Unsalted/unroasted nuts and seeds
- Fruits
- Fresh herbs
- Water
- Herbal tea
- Unsweetened non-dairy milks
- Extra virgin olive oil

ELIMINATE

- Gluten (wheat, rye, barley)
- Animal products (fish, eggs, meat)
- Caffeine, alcohol, soda
- Added sugar
- Dairy
- Processed or fried foods

plant-based treats

PROTEIN BALLS

These no bake balls offer a protein punch and are great on-the-go. Enjoy as a snack, dessert, or breakfast.

INGREDIENTS:
1 cup dates, pitted
½ cup rolled oats
¼ cup chia seeds
⅓ cup vegan chocolate chips
¼ cup vegan protein powder
¼ cup unsweetened shredded coconut
3 tablespoons almond butter

DIRECTIONS:
Place all ingredients in a food processor or blender. Mix until it forms a dough. Roll into balls. Store in the fridge or freezer.

CHIA SEED PUDDING

Chia seeds are a source of antioxidants, rich in fiber, omega-3 fats, protein, vitamins, minerals, and essential fatty acids.

INGREDIENTS:
3 cups unsweetened almond milk
½ cup chia seeds

DIRECTIONS:
Whisk the almond milk and chia seeds. Let sit for 5–10 minutes and then whisk again. Cover and chill in the fridge for 2.5–3 hours, or overnight. Stir well before serving. Add toppings such as granola, diced fruit, nuts, or seeds.

KALE CHIPS

Kale is nutrient dense with protein and iron, a great source of fiber, and full of vitamins A, C, and K.

INGREDIENTS:
a large bag of kale
extra virgin olive oil
nutritional yeast

DIRECTIONS:
Preheat the oven to 350 degrees. Remove leaves from the stalks, wash and dry in a salad spinner, and massage ½ tablespoon of extra virgin olive oil into the leaves. Spread them out on a baking sheet. Add Montreal steak seasoning or nutritional yeast. Bake 15 minutes or until crisp.

GREEN SMOOTHIE

This smoothie is high in fiber, low in sugar, and rich in vitamins and healthy fats.

INGREDIENTS:
½ cup vegan protein powder
2 handfuls spinach
1 tablespoon chia seeds
1 cup almond milk or water
½ avocado
1 tablespoon coconut oil
assorted frozen fruit
1 tablespoon ground flaxseed
½ banana

DIRECTIONS:
Combine all ingredients in a blender.

AVOCADO TOAST

Avocado has protein and healthy fat plus is high in fiber, potassium, vitamins B, C, E, and K.

INGREDIENTS:
bread
avocado
extra virgin olive oil

DIRECTIONS:
Slice and toast bread, drizzle with olive oil, and mash half an avocado on top with a fork. Top with Montreal steak seasoning, arugula, peaches, tomatoes, pine nuts, chili flakes, or chia seeds.

CRISPY CAULIFLOWER

Cauliflower is full of nutrients, high in fiber, and has anti-inflammatory benefits.

INGREDIENTS:
1 head of cauliflower cut into florets
1 tablespoon of extra virgin olive oil
¼ teaspoon black pepper
¼ teaspoon paprika
¼ teaspoon turmeric

DIRECTIONS:
Preheat the oven to 450 degrees. Toss cauliflower in oil and other ingredients. Spread the florets out evenly on a metal baking sheet. Bake for 20–30 minutes until a crispy golden brown. Enjoy with buffalo wing sauce.

capsule dressing

6 + 11

3 + 10

2 + 9

Make daily dress-up tranquil with a few timeless essentials that mix and match. **TIPS:** Going monochromatic offers a chic look, ensures everything matches, and can be easily dressed up or down. Top with a colorful scarf, strands of faux pearls, vintage earrings, red lips, and a dab of parfum.

Tune into *Tranquility du Jour* podcasts #259 and #310 for more on capsule dressing. Learn more at TranquiliT.com/capsule. See Style + Beauty (p. 74).

1: BOYFRIEND TANK
2: 2IN1 FITTED
3: BLAZER
4: LONG SLEEVE WRAP TUNIC
5: SLIP DRESS
6: SHIFT DRESS
7: LONG SLEEVE FULL SKIRT WRAP DRESS
8: SKIRT DRESS
9: LEGGING
10: PANTALON
11: PALAZZO PANT

MY 11 STAPLES ARE:

1. _____
2. _____
3. _____
4. _____
5. _____
6. _____
7. _____
8. _____
9. _____
10. _____
11. _____

WAYS TO MIX AND MATCH:

1. _____
2. _____
3. _____
4. _____
5. _____
6. _____
7. _____
8. _____

tranquil travel

"TRAVEL BRINGS POWER AND LOVE BACK INTO YOUR LIFE." —RUMI

TIPS:
1. Wear your bulkiest items when you travel.
2. Roll your clothing.
3. Pack products that serve multiple purposes such as Dr. Bronner's, shampoo/soap, and body/face moisturizer.
4. Pack versatile pieces that can be worn in multiple ways such as a skirt that can also be a dress.

TWO-WEEK PACKING LIST:
- Swimsuit
- Five pairs undies
- Two bras
- Three pairs of versatile shoes
- Five neutral-colored pants and/or shorts
- Three neutral-colored dresses and/or skirts
- Five neutral-colored tops
- Sun hat or beanie
- One–two colorful scarves
- One coat/jacket
- Socks and/or tights

TOOLS:
- Travel yoga mat
- Scented candle and lighter
- Earplugs and eye mask
- Lavender oil and parfum
- Assortment of teas and treats
- Reusable water bottle
- Pain reliever pills
- Journal and pens
- Camera and/or smartphone
- Chargers
- Travel-size toiletries: soap, shampoo, conditioner, deodorant, moisturizer
- Razor and tweezers
- Band-aids
- Face oil, mascara, lipstick
- Slippers
- Travel-size packet of detergent
- Headphones
- Passport
- Books
- Travel guides

MY TRAVEL MUST-HAVES:

TRANQUIL TRAVEL   39

monthly budget

EXPENSES

HOUSING
Rent/Mortgage $ _____
{   } $ _____
{   } $ _____

UTILITIES
Electricity $ _____
Water $ _____
Gas $ _____
Cable/Internet $ _____
Phone $ _____
{   } $ _____
{   } $ _____
{   } $ _____

TRANSPORTATION
Fuel $ _____
Insurance $ _____
Car Payment $ _____
Maintenance $ _____
{   } $ _____
{   } $ _____

FOOD
Groceries $ _____
Dining Out $ _____

MEDICAL
Premiums $ _____
Co-pays $ _____
Pharmacy $ _____
{   } $ _____
{   } $ _____

PERSONAL
Clothing $ _____
Entertainment $ _____
{   } $ _____
{   } $ _____
{   } $ _____
{   } $ _____

DEBT/LOANS
{   } $ _____
{   } $ _____
{   } $ _____
{   } $ _____
{   } $ _____

TOTAL $ _____

INCOME
Income #1 $ _____
Income #2 $ _____
{   } $ _____

TOTAL $ _____

GIVING
{   } $ _____
{   } $ _____
{   } $ _____

TOTAL $ _____

SAVINGS
Emergency $ _____
Retirement $ _____
{   } $ _____

TOTAL $ _____

weekly spending

WEEK OF: _____   **INCOME:** _____   **BUDGET:** _____

	SUNDAY	MONDAY	TUESDAY	WEDNESDAY	THURSDAY	FRIDAY	SATURDAY
RENT/MORTGAGE							
ELECTRICITY							
WATER							
GAS							
CABLE/INTERNET							
PHONE							
CAR FUEL							
CAR INSURANCE							
CAR LOAN							
CAR MAINTENANCE							
GROCERIES							
DINING OUT							
MEDICAL INSURANCE							
CO-PAYS							
PHARMACY							
CLOTHING							
ENTERTAINMENT							
DEBT/LOAN PAYMENTS							
CHARITABLE GIVING							
TOTAL							

observations:

PINK PEONIES, PILES OF BOOKS, ROSE GOLD, AND CUPS OF TEA.

30 days of tranquility

TRY THIS 30-DAY CHALLENGE TO INFUSE YOUR MONTH WITH SIMPLE PLEASURES.

1. SIT STILL FOR FIVE MINUTES
2. DO SIX SUN SALUTATIONS
3. WRITE A LOVE LETTER
4. APOLOGIZE
5. TELL THE TRUTH
6. CONSUME A GREEN DRINK
7. GO MEAT-FREE
8. WALK FOR 20 MINUTES
9. DO LEGS UP THE WALL
10. GIVE $10 TO CHARITY
11. PEN TWO JOURNAL PAGES
12. REVIEW YOUR YEAR'S DREAMS
13. CLEAR CLUTTER
14. GO ON AN ARTIST DATE
15. COLLAGE TWO PAGES
16. TREAT YOURSELF TO TEA
17. READ FOR 20 MINUTES
18. BUY YOURSELF FLOWERS
19. DANCE TO A FAVORITE TUNE
20. EXPRESS GRATITUDE
21. EAT ONLY UNPROCESSED FOODS
22. SOAK IN A BUBBLE BATH
23. MINDFULLY SIP A LIBATION
24. GET OUT IN NATURE
25. FORGO COMPLAINING
26. TAKE A DIGITAL DAY OFF
27. SNAP PHOTOS FROM YOUR DAY
28. MAKE A FAVORITE MEAL
29. HUG
30. BE FULLY PRESENT

monthly planner

MONTH: _____   INTENTION: _____

SUNDAY	MONDAY	TUESDAY	WEDNESDAY	THURSDAY	FRIDAY	SATURDAY

monthly tranquility tools and practices

- ○ CRAFT MONTH'S DREAMS
- ○ REVIEW BUDGET
- ○ WEEK 1
- ○ CREATE SOMETHING
- ○ READ TWO BOOKS
- ○ WEEK 2
- ○ VOLUNTEER
- ○ MANI/PEDI
- ○ WEEK 3
- ○ ENTERTAIN
- ○ MASSAGE
- ○ WEEK 4

month's dreams

DOODLE, LIST, COLLAGE, OR WRITE WHAT YOU'D LIKE TO MANIFEST THIS MONTH.

month's review

REVISIT YOUR MONTH'S DREAMS AND NOTE HOW THEY UNFOLDED FOR YOU.

moon phases

Notice your connection to the moon's cycles in these four phases: new, waxing, full, waning. Consider the prompts below as a way to tie into your Month's Dreams and provide space for monthly reflection. Tune into Tranquility du Jour podcast #424 Moon Wisdom.

new moon

A TIME FOR SETTING INTENTIONS.
I WANT . . .

waxing moon

A TIME FOR ACTION.
I WILL . . .

full moon

A TIME FOR HARVEST AND CLOSURE.
I RELEASE . . .

waning moon

A TIME FOR SOFTENING.
I FEEL . . .

daily checklist

TRACK YOUR INCORPORATION OF THE DAILY TRANQUILITY TOOLS.

1
- MORNING ROUTINE
- DAILY DRESS-UP
- MINDFUL MOVEMENT
- EAT YOUR VEGGIES
- JOURNAL
- GOAL REVIEW
- GRATITUDE
- EVENING ROUTINE
- ____________

2
- MORNING ROUTINE
- DAILY DRESS-UP
- MINDFUL MOVEMENT
- EAT YOUR VEGGIES
- JOURNAL
- GOAL REVIEW
- GRATITUDE
- EVENING ROUTINE
- ____________

3
- MORNING ROUTINE
- DAILY DRESS-UP
- MINDFUL MOVEMENT
- EAT YOUR VEGGIES
- JOURNAL
- GOAL REVIEW
- GRATITUDE
- EVENING ROUTINE
- ____________

4
- MORNING ROUTINE
- DAILY DRESS-UP
- MINDFUL MOVEMENT
- EAT YOUR VEGGIES
- JOURNAL
- GOAL REVIEW
- GRATITUDE
- EVENING ROUTINE
- ____________

5
- MORNING ROUTINE
- DAILY DRESS-UP
- MINDFUL MOVEMENT
- EAT YOUR VEGGIES
- JOURNAL
- GOAL REVIEW
- GRATITUDE
- EVENING ROUTINE
- ____________

6
- MORNING ROUTINE
- DAILY DRESS-UP
- MINDFUL MOVEMENT
- EAT YOUR VEGGIES
- JOURNAL
- GOAL REVIEW
- GRATITUDE
- EVENING ROUTINE
- ____________

7
- MORNING ROUTINE
- DAILY DRESS-UP
- MINDFUL MOVEMENT
- EAT YOUR VEGGIES
- JOURNAL
- GOAL REVIEW
- GRATITUDE
- EVENING ROUTINE
- ____________

8
- MORNING ROUTINE
- DAILY DRESS-UP
- MINDFUL MOVEMENT
- EAT YOUR VEGGIES
- JOURNAL
- GOAL REVIEW
- GRATITUDE
- EVENING ROUTINE
- ____________

9
- MORNING ROUTINE
- DAILY DRESS-UP
- MINDFUL MOVEMENT
- EAT YOUR VEGGIES
- JOURNAL
- GOAL REVIEW
- GRATITUDE
- EVENING ROUTINE
- ____________

10
- MORNING ROUTINE
- DAILY DRESS-UP
- MINDFUL MOVEMENT
- EAT YOUR VEGGIES
- JOURNAL
- GOAL REVIEW
- GRATITUDE
- EVENING ROUTINE
- ____________

11
- MORNING ROUTINE
- DAILY DRESS-UP
- MINDFUL MOVEMENT
- EAT YOUR VEGGIES
- JOURNAL
- GOAL REVIEW
- GRATITUDE
- EVENING ROUTINE
- ____________

12
- MORNING ROUTINE
- DAILY DRESS-UP
- MINDFUL MOVEMENT
- EAT YOUR VEGGIES
- JOURNAL
- GOAL REVIEW
- GRATITUDE
- EVENING ROUTINE
- ____________

13
- MORNING ROUTINE
- DAILY DRESS-UP
- MINDFUL MOVEMENT
- EAT YOUR VEGGIES
- JOURNAL
- GOAL REVIEW
- GRATITUDE
- EVENING ROUTINE
- ____________

14
- MORNING ROUTINE
- DAILY DRESS-UP
- MINDFUL MOVEMENT
- EAT YOUR VEGGIES
- JOURNAL
- GOAL REVIEW
- GRATITUDE
- EVENING ROUTINE
- ____________

15
- MORNING ROUTINE
- DAILY DRESS-UP
- MINDFUL MOVEMENT
- EAT YOUR VEGGIES
- JOURNAL
- GOAL REVIEW
- GRATITUDE
- EVENING ROUTINE
- ____________

16
- MORNING ROUTINE
- DAILY DRESS-UP
- MINDFUL MOVEMENT
- EAT YOUR VEGGIES
- JOURNAL
- GOAL REVIEW
- GRATITUDE
- EVENING ROUTINE
- ____________

17
- MORNING ROUTINE
- DAILY DRESS-UP
- MINDFUL MOVEMENT
- EAT YOUR VEGGIES
- JOURNAL
- GOAL REVIEW
- GRATITUDE
- EVENING ROUTINE
- ____________

18
- MORNING ROUTINE
- DAILY DRESS-UP
- MINDFUL MOVEMENT
- EAT YOUR VEGGIES
- JOURNAL
- GOAL REVIEW
- GRATITUDE
- EVENING ROUTINE
- ____________

19
- MORNING ROUTINE
- DAILY DRESS-UP
- MINDFUL MOVEMENT
- EAT YOUR VEGGIES
- JOURNAL
- GOAL REVIEW
- GRATITUDE
- EVENING ROUTINE
- ____________

20
- MORNING ROUTINE
- DAILY DRESS-UP
- MINDFUL MOVEMENT
- EAT YOUR VEGGIES
- JOURNAL
- GOAL REVIEW
- GRATITUDE
- EVENING ROUTINE
- ____________

21
- MORNING ROUTINE
- DAILY DRESS-UP
- MINDFUL MOVEMENT
- EAT YOUR VEGGIES
- JOURNAL
- GOAL REVIEW
- GRATITUDE
- EVENING ROUTINE
- ____________

22
- MORNING ROUTINE
- DAILY DRESS-UP
- MINDFUL MOVEMENT
- EAT YOUR VEGGIES
- JOURNAL
- GOAL REVIEW
- GRATITUDE
- EVENING ROUTINE
- ____________

23
- MORNING ROUTINE
- DAILY DRESS-UP
- MINDFUL MOVEMENT
- EAT YOUR VEGGIES
- JOURNAL
- GOAL REVIEW
- GRATITUDE
- EVENING ROUTINE
- ____________

24
- MORNING ROUTINE
- DAILY DRESS-UP
- MINDFUL MOVEMENT
- EAT YOUR VEGGIES
- JOURNAL
- GOAL REVIEW
- GRATITUDE
- EVENING ROUTINE
- ____________

25
- MORNING ROUTINE
- DAILY DRESS-UP
- MINDFUL MOVEMENT
- EAT YOUR VEGGIES
- JOURNAL
- GOAL REVIEW
- GRATITUDE
- EVENING ROUTINE
- ____________

26
- MORNING ROUTINE
- DAILY DRESS-UP
- MINDFUL MOVEMENT
- EAT YOUR VEGGIES
- JOURNAL
- GOAL REVIEW
- GRATITUDE
- EVENING ROUTINE
- ____________

27
- MORNING ROUTINE
- DAILY DRESS-UP
- MINDFUL MOVEMENT
- EAT YOUR VEGGIES
- JOURNAL
- GOAL REVIEW
- GRATITUDE
- EVENING ROUTINE
- ____________

28
- MORNING ROUTINE
- DAILY DRESS-UP
- MINDFUL MOVEMENT
- EAT YOUR VEGGIES
- JOURNAL
- GOAL REVIEW
- GRATITUDE
- EVENING ROUTINE
- ____________

29
- MORNING ROUTINE
- DAILY DRESS-UP
- MINDFUL MOVEMENT
- EAT YOUR VEGGIES
- JOURNAL
- GOAL REVIEW
- GRATITUDE
- EVENING ROUTINE
- ____________

30
- MORNING ROUTINE
- DAILY DRESS-UP
- MINDFUL MOVEMENT
- EAT YOUR VEGGIES
- JOURNAL
- GOAL REVIEW
- GRATITUDE
- EVENING ROUTINE
- ____________

dreams

"THE WORLD NEEDS DREAMERS AND THE WORLD NEEDS DOERS, BUT MOST OF ALL THE WORLD NEEDS DREAMERS WHO DO."
—SARAH BAN BREATHNACH

When I first read this quote, I was in my mid-20s and disenchanted with an unhealthy relationship and a paralegal job at a Washington, DC, law firm. As I do with most books, I underlined and highlighted numerous passages that spoke to me. The one above, by the author of Simple Abundance, *has stuck with me for nearly two decades. It succinctly describes the yin and yang of being and doing.*

The new year (or new day for those of you starting any other time) often begins with a pile of resolutions and intentions that may be forgotten by midmonth. While I'm not one to squash hopes for the new year, I'm one to encourage a blend of dreaming and doing—a little head in the clouds mixed with a little feet on the ground.

To begin exploring your dreams, consider a word or theme for the year. Reflect on what you'd like more/less of in your life, how you want to feel, and what you need. Capture what comes up and make a list of possible words or themes like beauty, slowing down, or moving on.

Next, list your Year's Dreams (p. 22)—this is everything you hope for the year ahead. What do you want and need? Note places to visit, recipes to try, habits to stop, people to see, books to read, events to host or attend, and practices to start, along with the nitty gritty like financial goals such as saving to buy a home. This process serves as a helpful guidepost throughout the year, especially when circling back 12 months later to review it.

Review your dreams to see if there's a theme or word that's running through them. If so, go with it! If not, return to your word or theme list and notice what word evokes an exhale or a spark of joy. That's the word! It will serve as an anchor or road map for the year. For example, when struggling with a decision, ask yourself, "Does this look like beauty/slowing down/moving on?" Consider how applying this word or theme to all areas of your life would look. This, too, may help with creating your Year's Dreams.

Creating the list of dreams takes some soul searching mixed with right brain thinking and is our planting season. When you're ready, create action steps to bring them to life. Design them to be SMART: specific, measurable, achievable, relevant, time-bound. This uses left brain thinking and is our growing period where adequate watering of the seeds is necessary. Both stages are necessary. Not all seeds will grow and that's okay. Some may need more time to germinate.

I call this process reflection, intention, and action and follow it every year. I'll carve out a few quiet hours, gather a sketchbook and markers, and settle in. I begin with reflecting on the previous year: lessons learned, adventures, accomplishments, losses, how time and energy were spent. Looking through photos and my planner helps me remember those forgotten experiences.

From there, I'll set an intention for the new year by choosing my theme and listing my dreams such as eat less sugar, take 12 ballet classes each month, make weekly dates with friends, and host three Pigs & Pugs events. Next comes the action of monitoring my sugar intake, putting classes into my planner (and going to them), reaching out to friends to make dates, and coordinating event planning with my non-profit board.

The post-action steps include monitoring the actions and modifying, as needed. For example, perhaps three Pigs & Pugs events is too much, 12 ballet classes is too few, or monthly versus weekly dates with friends is more doable. No problem, simply readjust according to what feels realistic to you right now. And don't forget to celebrate those successes—especially the little ones. Skipped added sugar in your latte? Good job! Hosted an event that raised $500 for charity? Amazing!

What does reflection, intention, and action look like for you?

It may not be that you need to create any new dreams right now; it may be that you need to shed something that isn't working anymore. Similar to how a snake sheds its skin so that it can grow, sometimes we, too, need to shed ours to make room for our own growth.

At times, we can get stuck in the muddy middle. We've said goodbye to an old dream such as a business, relationship, job, or city, and we're in an in-between stage. We may not be quite ready to jump headfirst into a new dream, but rather need time and space to mourn our old one and consider its lessons before moving on. Honor that time of being fallow and hold yourself tenderly during it; you're making space for what's to come.

As poet Rainer Maria Rilke said, "Be patient toward all that is unsolved in your heart and try to love the questions themselves, like locked rooms and like books that are now written in a very foreign tongue. Do not now seek the answers, which cannot be given you because you would not be able to live them. And the point is, to live everything."

What's on your Year's Dreams list? Review what you've written to make sure you've captured everything you want to savor this year. Now, picture yourself living a life of deep meaning. What are you doing and where? Who are you with? How do you feel? Compare it to your life right now. No judgment, just notice. What's different? What's similar?

Are there any pieces from that ideal life vision that you'd like to add to your Year's Dreams? If so, add them! If not, it looks like you've gotten fairly clear, congrats!

Shortly after reading *Simple Abundance*, I left the painful relationship, picked up *The Artist's Way*, launched a yoga studio in my living room, and became my own boss. How? By following these steps in pursuit of my dreams that continue to evolve as I grow.

American statesman Paul Nitze wrote, "One of the most dangerous forms of human error is forgetting what one is trying to achieve." Live your word/theme of the year. Stay connected to your dreams. Honor your progress. Shift course, as needed. Encourage your growth. Be gentle with yourself. Fight the good fight. Celebrate your successes. Let's bring our dreams to life and make a difference!

savvy sources

BOOKS:
Make Your Creative Dreams Real by SARK
Write it Down, Make it Happen by Henriette Anne Klauser
A Book That Takes Its Time by Irene Smit
The Crossroads of Should and Must by Elle Luna
The Desire Map by Danielle LaPorte
Simple Abundance by Sarah Ban Breathnach

APPS:
Fabulous
BucketListly

TRANQUILITY DU JOUR PODCASTS:
#95 Scheduling and Time Management
#117 The Power of Writing Things Down
#211 Dreams to Reality
#313 Procrastination to Creative Genius
#396 Start Right Where You Are

1

WEEK 1: YEAR'S DREAMS

List what you'd like to manifest in the new year. Is it weekly social time? How about returning to a former passion like dance or painting? Do you want to invest 5 percent of your income? Is graduate school beckoning? Will you finish writing that novel?

When you picture yourself at the end of the year, what do you want to have seen, felt, experienced, and/or accomplished?

Circle your top five to 10 dreams and list three tiny action steps (aka micromovements) to help bring that dream to life. Make your micromovements SMART. For example, "I'll finish my online veterinary social work classes by March 15." Micromovements would be to log in to the curriculum, write study time into your planner, and read through the first lesson.

weekly tranquility tools

- ○ PLAN WEEK'S MITS
- ○ PEN A LOVE NOTE
- ○ SOAK IN THE TUB
- ○ ARTIST DATE
- ○ DIGITAL DAY OFF
- ○ GREEN JUICE
- ○ CLEAR CLUTTER
- ○ BUY OR PICK FRESH FLOWERS

WEEK 2: REACHING YOUR DREAMS

To increase your likelihood of achieving your goals, consider working with an accountability partner, writing a contract, using primers, and creating an if/then scenario.

A 1994 study by Schlenker, et al., found that participants who reported their progress on a task scored 243 percent higher than those who had no accountability. Set up an accountability partnership and share your Year's Dreams' progress with a supportive confidant.

Creating a written contract helped increase participants' probability of meeting a goal by 86 percent in a 2009 study by Miller & Frisch. Try writing a contract to yourself noting a micromovement you want to take. For example, I, (your name), commit to sitting in meditation 10 minutes a day.

Primers are cues used to help us stay connected to our dreams on a daily basis. Post sticky notes with reminders such as "eat your greens." Wear a charm bracelet with trinkets of a place you want to visit like the Eiffel Tower. Attach your vision board to your refrigerator. Create a password that reiterates your goal, "DreamsOfIndia." Use a screensaver with an image of a woman in nature if your goal is to hike the Grand Canyon.

Create an if/then scenario to triple the chances of success, such as, "If I'm tempted to hit the vending machine midday, then I'll go for a walk around the building and pick up a healthy snack nearby."

weekly tranquility tools

- PLAN WEEK'S MITS
- PEN A LOVE NOTE
- SOAK IN THE TUB
- ARTIST DATE
- DIGITAL DAY OFF
- GREEN JUICE
- CLEAR CLUTTER
- BUY OR PICK FRESH FLOWERS

MY LIFE IS MY ART.

WEEK 3: VISUALIZE YOUR DREAMS

Contemplate what images would represent those top five to 10 dreams. This can help you when searching the internet for images to print (or put into an online collage if you'd rather go digital). It can also assist you in determining what genre of magazines you'd like to gather.

Cull through your resources to find images that speak to you and bring your dreams into visual form. Then lay the images out on a file folder, in your planner, your journal, or on your refrigerator. Add words. You can find perfect slogans in magazines. Move them around until you find the collage look you love. Next, set the images with glue or washi tape.

Add your word or theme of the year to the collage. Can't find the whole word? Cut out letters and create your word.

weekly tranquility tools

- PLAN WEEK'S MITS
- PEN A LOVE NOTE
- SOAK IN THE TUB
- ARTIST DATE
- DIGITAL DAY OFF
- GREEN JUICE
- CLEAR CLUTTER
- BUY OR PICK FRESH FLOWERS

WEEK 4: CRAFT A LETTER

Picture yourself a year from today having accomplished or having taken steps toward accomplishing your Year's Dreams. How do you feel? Where are you? What are you doing? What are you eating? Who are you with? What are you wearing?

Pen yourself a letter to open a year from now and write it in the present tense. For example, "I'm so glad you made self-care a priority this year. You are now sleeping through the night, eating more whole foods, and doing yoga three times a week." Keep going. Bring those micromovements to life here and dream about how life will look once you make yourself and your goals a priority this year.

INSTRUCTIONS: Write your letter on the following page and date it a year from today. Cut it out and seal it in an envelope of your choice. Using washi tape, stick it onto A Letter To My Future Self (p. 220).

weekly tranquility tools

- ○ PLAN WEEK'S MITS
- ○ PEN A LOVE NOTE
- ○ SOAK IN THE TUB
- ○ ARTIST DATE
- ○ DIGITAL DAY OFF
- ○ GREEN JUICE
- ○ CLEAR CLUTTER
- ○ BUY OR PICK FRESH FLOWERS

a letter to my future self

date _____

dear _____,

monthly planner

MONTH: _____ INTENTION: _____

SUNDAY	MONDAY	TUESDAY	WEDNESDAY	THURSDAY	FRIDAY	SATURDAY

monthly tranquility tools and practices

- ○ CRAFT MONTH'S DREAMS
- ○ REVIEW BUDGET
- ○ WEEK 1

- ○ CREATE SOMETHING
- ○ READ TWO BOOKS
- ○ WEEK 2

- ○ VOLUNTEER
- ○ MANI/PEDI
- ○ WEEK 3

- ○ ENTERTAIN
- ○ MASSAGE
- ○ WEEK 4

month's dreams

month's review

moon phases

Notice your connection to the moon's cycles in these four phases: new, waxing, full, waning. Consider the prompts below as a way to tie into your Month's Dreams and provide space for monthly reflection.

new moon

A TIME FOR SETTING INTENTIONS.
I WANT . . .

waxing moon

A TIME FOR ACTION.
I WILL . . .

full moon

A TIME FOR HARVEST AND CLOSURE.
I RELEASE . . .

waning moon

A TIME FOR SOFTENING.
I FEEL . . .

daily checklist

TRACK YOUR INCORPORATION OF THE DAILY TRANQUILITY TOOLS.

For each of days 1 through 30, the following checklist is repeated:

- ○ MORNING ROUTINE
- ○ DAILY DRESS-UP
- ○ MINDFUL MOVEMENT
- ○ EAT YOUR VEGGIES
- ○ JOURNAL
- ○ GOAL REVIEW
- ○ GRATITUDE
- ○ EVENING ROUTINE
- ○ _____

love

"CLOSE YOUR EYES. FALL IN LOVE. STAY THERE." —RUMI

Ah, Rumi, he gets me every time. Let's explore ways to infuse our days with more love, shall we? I believe there's a strong connection to how we feel about others and ourselves that, ultimately, affects how satisfied we are with our lives.

When you hear love, what comes to mind? Cupid, families, roses, commitment ceremonies, walks on the beach, heart-shaped hot tubs? We all have an assortment of ideas around what love means, so let's see what the dictionary has to say.

The Oxford dictionary defines love as "an intense feeling of deep affection." With that in mind, think about the various things that you love. Possibly chocolate, a family member, a good friend, chamomile tea, stargazing . . . and the list can go on and on.

Love shows up in a myriad of ways and doesn't have to involve another person. As the Rumi quote above reminds us, we find love within. This month we'll focus on both by deepening the love we have for ourselves and deepening the ways that we share love with the world.

Self-love is not a narcissistic trait; instead it's taking care of our well-being and overall happiness. It's critical to our health! When I think back on my inability to set boundaries in my early 20s, I now see that as a lack of self-love. Eager to please, I was involved in relationships (romantic and otherwise) that didn't contribute to my wellness and instead depleted my energy resources.

Over the years, I've become much more cautious with myself. This came with getting to know myself better, recognizing I was an introvert and needed lots of replenishment time, and being slower to share my time. Self-love grows from making decisions and taking actions to support ourselves. It starts with self-awareness.

There is no prescription for this process. It's a lifelong journey, and it's never too late to start down the path toward self-love. By accepting ourselves—eccentricities and all—our lifelong romance deepens. It also makes us more appealing to others.

Now let's talk about others—community, friends, lovers, family, pets, causes, colleagues, and more! I've always been a fan of the little things. From setting up a scavenger hunt for a loved one, to remembering friends' birthdays, to putting love notes in a suitcase for my partner to open while on travel, to sending snail mail care packages. I'll even turn on classical music for my pugs to enjoy when I'm gone. These are ways I show love. What about you?

There are so many ways to give love to others that go well beyond my small examples above. Relationship expert John Gottman developed the Six Magic Hours as a formula to deepen our romantic relationships. Since we have 168, six hours per week doesn't sound too far-fetched and includes mindful partings and reunions, appreciation and admiration, affection, a two-hour date night, and a one-hour state of the union meeting.

While that notion was developed for couples, it's a handy way to think about all of our relationships. Our comings and goings (think of the person you pass in the office on Monday morning), sharing appreciation, and spending time help build all of our relationships and, ultimately, deepen our love and connection.

This level of compassion is best extended to all beings, including human, furry, scaly, and feathery. Adopt or sponsor an animal. Forgo products made with palm oil or animals. Try Meatless Mondays. Purchase cruelty-free cosmetics and household products. Support compassionate fashion. Visit and support animal sanctuaries. Volunteer at a shelter or rescue. Boycott puppy mills and fur. Foster a pet. The list goes on and on.

After all, compassion is the new black. Remember we always have a choice. Ask yourself throughout the day, "What would it look like to choose love right now?" And why not be your very own Valentine every single day?

Savvy Sources

BOOKS:
Big Love by Scott Stabile
Madly in Love with Me by Christine Arylo
Succulent Wild Love by SARK
The Mastery of Love by Don Miguel Ruiz
A Return to Love by Marianne Williamson
Girl, Wash Your Face by Rachel Hollis
The Relationship Cure by John Gottman and Joan DeClaire

APPS:
Gottman Card Decks
Kindness

TRANQUILITY DU JOUR PODCASTS:
#22 Mindful Relationships
#62 Refined Relations
#156 Musings on Self-Love
#230 Friendship Fix
#270 Relationships + Tiny Living
#362 Succulent Wild Love
#408 Big Love

1

WEEK 1: SELF-LOVE

Oscar Wilde said, "To love oneself is the beginning of a lifelong romance." My hope is that this month's practices help you fall more in love with yourself—eccentricities and all!

To get us started, consider your relationship with yourself. What are some of the ways you currently "romance" you?

To romance yourself in big and small ways, consider these practices: set boundaries, notice what you need, be your own cheerleader, acknowledge your emotions (notice the sensations, name the emotion, navigate the experience with awareness), move your body, eat whole foods, study to deepen your understanding, feel sunshine on your skin, surround yourself with beauty, enjoy inspiring music and films, visit museums and art galleries, savor the performing arts, express your creativity, avoid comparisons, observe your mind chatter and replace negative thoughts, buy yourself flowers, step beyond your comfort zone, take a mental health day, do what you enjoy, focus on what you can change, work with a therapist or coach, forgive, forgo perfection, manage your energy, let go of toxic relationships, start a "good things jar" where you note what went well that day, date it and put it in a Mason jar.

End your day with love by unwinding in a way that nurtures your soul: spend time with loved ones, work on a project that brings joy, reflect on the day, celebrate your wins, express gratitude, read, savor a nourishing drink, stretch your body, shift your mindset from, "I have so much to do," to "I did my best today and tomorrow is a new day."

Note the ones you do regularly and acknowledge yourself for them!

List any that you would enjoy and can make time for over the next few months and get something scheduled such as a hike, art exhibit, or massage. Choose one new way to deepen your romantic relationship with yourself this week. Make a date with yourself. Write it in your planner. Put on an outfit you love, spritz perfume, and head to your favorite vegan restaurant, museum, or bookstore café.

weekly tranquility tools

- ○ PLAN WEEK'S MITS
- ○ PEN A LOVE NOTE
- ○ SOAK IN THE TUB
- ○ ARTIST DATE
- ○ DIGITAL DAY OFF
- ○ GREEN JUICE
- ○ CLEAR CLUTTER
- ○ BUY OR PICK FRESH FLOWERS

WEEK 2: NURTURING RELATIONSHIPS

Choose a relationship or two you want to nurture. Focus on spreading love simply by being you.

Here are some ideas: ask how you can support someone, apologize and ask how you can make it better, keep your phone tucked away when in conversation, bake something for your team, volunteer at a local shelter, adopt a rescue pet, hold the door for the person behind you, say thank you, smile, write a letter, think loving thoughts, treat someone to tea, recycle, remember that hurt people hurt other people and embrace compassion, let someone into your lane, make a gift for someone going through a hard time, make date nights with friends.

Give yourself a pat on the back for the ones you already do. List any that you would enjoy and can make time for over the next few months and get something scheduled such as teatime, volunteering, or being present. Make a brunch date and listen intently to what's said. Try one new idea this week.

weekly tranquility tools

- PLAN WEEK'S MITS
- PEN A LOVE NOTE
- SOAK IN THE TUB
- ARTIST DATE
- DIGITAL DAY OFF
- GREEN JUICE
- CLEAR CLUTTER
- BUY OR PICK FRESH FLOWERS

WEEK 3: MINDFUL SELF-COMPASSION

Self-compassion is treating ourselves with the same love we'd show a friend. It's also been described as treating ourselves as tenderly as a parent would treat a child with the flu. Can't you just feel the compassion and tenderness flowing from that image?!

According to the co-creator of Mindful Self-Compassion, Kristin Neff, the three practices of self-compassion include:

1. **SELF-KINDNESS VS. SELF-JUDGMENT.** Self-kindness means treating mishaps with tenderness and acknowledging that perfection is unattainable instead of ruminating on past mistakes.

2. **COMMON HUMANITY VS. ISOLATION.** Common humanity is recognition that all humans suffer and that we're not alone when we, too, struggle.

3. **MINDFULNESS VS. OVER-IDENTIFICATION.** Mindfulness is observing our thoughts and feelings without judging them as good or bad. Notice what arises and name the sensation while remembering that thoughts and emotions are like weather patterns, always in flux. For example, instead of labeling ourselves as angry, we acknowledge that we're experiencing anger in that moment.

Know that the more you accept yourself as you are, the more you can change. We need to name our emotions to tame them and feel them to heal them. What we resist persists. Labeling our difficult emotions calms the amygdala, which is part of the brain responsible for emotions, emotional behavior, and motivation.

If you find yourself frustrated or discouraged this week, offer yourself a generous dose of self-compassion. Treat yourself with kindness, recognize your common humanity, and/or practice mindfulness with your emotions.

weekly tranquility tools

- PLAN WEEK'S MITS
- PEN A LOVE NOTE
- SOAK IN THE TUB
- ARTIST DATE
- DIGITAL DAY OFF
- GREEN JUICE
- CLEAR CLUTTER
- BUY OR PICK FRESH FLOWERS

WEEK 4: LOVING-KINDNESS

The practice of loving-kindness (also called metta) is a focus on kindness, goodwill, and generosity. It helps us develop the mindset of loving acceptance toward others and ourselves.

Begin by silently repeating these phrases. Send loving-kindness to yourself with "May I . . ." Then choose a loved one and someone who is struggling by silently repeating, "May you . . ." You can also add in someone who is neutral to you (the bus driver, barista, neighbor you don't know) and someone who you're having difficulty with right now.

You'll find numerous phrases available; below are my favorite four.

May I be happy.
May I be healthy.
May I have ease of body and mind.
May I be at peace.

May you be happy.
May you be healthy.
May you have ease of body and mind.
May you be at peace.

This practice has been linked to increased positivity, decreased chronic pain, increased gray matter in the brain, increased compassion, and decreased self-criticism.

Try practicing what's called street metta—the practice of taking loving-kindness off the meditation cushion and into the world to share it with others on the bus, in line, at the airport, stuck in traffic, etc.

This week practice loving-kindness—ideally every day for a few minutes either at home, at the office, or on-the-go. Observe your reactions, both physically and emotionally.

weekly tranquility tools

- PLAN WEEK'S MITS
- PEN A LOVE NOTE
- SOAK IN THE TUB
- ARTIST DATE
- DIGITAL DAY OFF
- GREEN JUICE
- CLEAR CLUTTER
- BUY OR PICK FRESH FLOWERS

monthly planner

MONTH: _____   INTENTION: _____

SUNDAY	MONDAY	TUESDAY	WEDNESDAY	THURSDAY	FRIDAY	SATURDAY

monthly tranquility tools and practices

- ○ CRAFT MONTH'S DREAMS
- ○ REVIEW BUDGET
- ○ WEEK 1

- ○ CREATE SOMETHING
- ○ READ TWO BOOKS
- ○ WEEK 2

- ○ VOLUNTEER
- ○ MANI/PEDI
- ○ WEEK 3

- ○ ENTERTAIN
- ○ MASSAGE
- ○ WEEK 4

month's dreams

month's review

moon phases

Notice your connection to the moon's cycles in these four phases: new, waxing, full, waning. Consider the prompts below as a way to tie into your Month's Dreams and provide space for monthly reflection.

new moon

waxing moon

A TIME FOR SETTING INTENTIONS.
I WANT . . .

A TIME FOR ACTION.
I WILL . . .

full moon

waning moon

A TIME FOR HARVEST AND CLOSURE.
I RELEASE . . .

A TIME FOR SOFTENING.
I FEEL . . .

daily checklist

TRACK YOUR INCORPORATION OF THE DAILY TRANQUILITY TOOLS.

○ MORNING ROUTINE ○ DAILY DRESS-UP ○ MINDFUL MOVEMENT ○ EAT YOUR VEGGIES ○ JOURNAL ○ GOAL REVIEW ○ GRATITUDE ○ EVENING ROUTINE ○ _____	○ MORNING ROUTINE ○ DAILY DRESS-UP ○ MINDFUL MOVEMENT ○ EAT YOUR VEGGIES ○ JOURNAL ○ GOAL REVIEW ○ GRATITUDE ○ EVENING ROUTINE ○ _____	○ MORNING ROUTINE ○ DAILY DRESS-UP ○ MINDFUL MOVEMENT ○ EAT YOUR VEGGIES ○ JOURNAL ○ GOAL REVIEW ○ GRATITUDE ○ EVENING ROUTINE ○ _____	○ MORNING ROUTINE ○ DAILY DRESS-UP ○ MINDFUL MOVEMENT ○ EAT YOUR VEGGIES ○ JOURNAL ○ GOAL REVIEW ○ GRATITUDE ○ EVENING ROUTINE ○ _____	○ MORNING ROUTINE ○ DAILY DRESS-UP ○ MINDFUL MOVEMENT ○ EAT YOUR VEGGIES ○ JOURNAL ○ GOAL REVIEW ○ GRATITUDE ○ EVENING ROUTINE ○ _____
○ MORNING ROUTINE ○ DAILY DRESS-UP ○ MINDFUL MOVEMENT ○ EAT YOUR VEGGIES ○ JOURNAL ○ GOAL REVIEW ○ GRATITUDE ○ EVENING ROUTINE ○ _____	○ MORNING ROUTINE ○ DAILY DRESS-UP ○ MINDFUL MOVEMENT ○ EAT YOUR VEGGIES ○ JOURNAL ○ GOAL REVIEW ○ GRATITUDE ○ EVENING ROUTINE ○ _____	○ MORNING ROUTINE ○ DAILY DRESS-UP ○ MINDFUL MOVEMENT ○ EAT YOUR VEGGIES ○ JOURNAL ○ GOAL REVIEW ○ GRATITUDE ○ EVENING ROUTINE ○ _____	○ MORNING ROUTINE ○ DAILY DRESS-UP ○ MINDFUL MOVEMENT ○ EAT YOUR VEGGIES ○ JOURNAL ○ GOAL REVIEW ○ GRATITUDE ○ EVENING ROUTINE ○ _____	○ MORNING ROUTINE ○ DAILY DRESS-UP ○ MINDFUL MOVEMENT ○ EAT YOUR VEGGIES ○ JOURNAL ○ GOAL REVIEW ○ GRATITUDE ○ EVENING ROUTINE ○ _____
○ MORNING ROUTINE ○ DAILY DRESS-UP ○ MINDFUL MOVEMENT ○ EAT YOUR VEGGIES ○ JOURNAL ○ GOAL REVIEW ○ GRATITUDE ○ EVENING ROUTINE ○ _____	○ MORNING ROUTINE ○ DAILY DRESS-UP ○ MINDFUL MOVEMENT ○ EAT YOUR VEGGIES ○ JOURNAL ○ GOAL REVIEW ○ GRATITUDE ○ EVENING ROUTINE ○ _____	○ MORNING ROUTINE ○ DAILY DRESS-UP ○ MINDFUL MOVEMENT ○ EAT YOUR VEGGIES ○ JOURNAL ○ GOAL REVIEW ○ GRATITUDE ○ EVENING ROUTINE ○ _____	○ MORNING ROUTINE ○ DAILY DRESS-UP ○ MINDFUL MOVEMENT ○ EAT YOUR VEGGIES ○ JOURNAL ○ GOAL REVIEW ○ GRATITUDE ○ EVENING ROUTINE ○ _____	○ MORNING ROUTINE ○ DAILY DRESS-UP ○ MINDFUL MOVEMENT ○ EAT YOUR VEGGIES ○ JOURNAL ○ GOAL REVIEW ○ GRATITUDE ○ EVENING ROUTINE ○ _____
○ MORNING ROUTINE ○ DAILY DRESS-UP ○ MINDFUL MOVEMENT ○ EAT YOUR VEGGIES ○ JOURNAL ○ GOAL REVIEW ○ GRATITUDE ○ EVENING ROUTINE ○ _____	○ MORNING ROUTINE ○ DAILY DRESS-UP ○ MINDFUL MOVEMENT ○ EAT YOUR VEGGIES ○ JOURNAL ○ GOAL REVIEW ○ GRATITUDE ○ EVENING ROUTINE ○ _____	○ MORNING ROUTINE ○ DAILY DRESS-UP ○ MINDFUL MOVEMENT ○ EAT YOUR VEGGIES ○ JOURNAL ○ GOAL REVIEW ○ GRATITUDE ○ EVENING ROUTINE ○ _____	○ MORNING ROUTINE ○ DAILY DRESS-UP ○ MINDFUL MOVEMENT ○ EAT YOUR VEGGIES ○ JOURNAL ○ GOAL REVIEW ○ GRATITUDE ○ EVENING ROUTINE ○ _____	○ MORNING ROUTINE ○ DAILY DRESS-UP ○ MINDFUL MOVEMENT ○ EAT YOUR VEGGIES ○ JOURNAL ○ GOAL REVIEW ○ GRATITUDE ○ EVENING ROUTINE ○ _____
○ MORNING ROUTINE ○ DAILY DRESS-UP ○ MINDFUL MOVEMENT ○ EAT YOUR VEGGIES ○ JOURNAL ○ GOAL REVIEW ○ GRATITUDE ○ EVENING ROUTINE ○ _____	○ MORNING ROUTINE ○ DAILY DRESS-UP ○ MINDFUL MOVEMENT ○ EAT YOUR VEGGIES ○ JOURNAL ○ GOAL REVIEW ○ GRATITUDE ○ EVENING ROUTINE ○ _____	○ MORNING ROUTINE ○ DAILY DRESS-UP ○ MINDFUL MOVEMENT ○ EAT YOUR VEGGIES ○ JOURNAL ○ GOAL REVIEW ○ GRATITUDE ○ EVENING ROUTINE ○ _____	○ MORNING ROUTINE ○ DAILY DRESS-UP ○ MINDFUL MOVEMENT ○ EAT YOUR VEGGIES ○ JOURNAL ○ GOAL REVIEW ○ GRATITUDE ○ EVENING ROUTINE ○ _____	○ MORNING ROUTINE ○ DAILY DRESS-UP ○ MINDFUL MOVEMENT ○ EAT YOUR VEGGIES ○ JOURNAL ○ GOAL REVIEW ○ GRATITUDE ○ EVENING ROUTINE ○ _____
○ MORNING ROUTINE ○ DAILY DRESS-UP ○ MINDFUL MOVEMENT ○ EAT YOUR VEGGIES ○ JOURNAL ○ GOAL REVIEW ○ GRATITUDE ○ EVENING ROUTINE ○ _____	○ MORNING ROUTINE ○ DAILY DRESS-UP ○ MINDFUL MOVEMENT ○ EAT YOUR VEGGIES ○ JOURNAL ○ GOAL REVIEW ○ GRATITUDE ○ EVENING ROUTINE ○ _____	○ MORNING ROUTINE ○ DAILY DRESS-UP ○ MINDFUL MOVEMENT ○ EAT YOUR VEGGIES ○ JOURNAL ○ GOAL REVIEW ○ GRATITUDE ○ EVENING ROUTINE ○ _____	○ MORNING ROUTINE ○ DAILY DRESS-UP ○ MINDFUL MOVEMENT ○ EAT YOUR VEGGIES ○ JOURNAL ○ GOAL REVIEW ○ GRATITUDE ○ EVENING ROUTINE ○ _____	○ MORNING ROUTINE ○ DAILY DRESS-UP ○ MINDFUL MOVEMENT ○ EAT YOUR VEGGIES ○ JOURNAL ○ GOAL REVIEW ○ GRATITUDE ○ EVENING ROUTINE ○ _____

style + beauty

"STYLE IS KNOWING WHO YOU ARE, WHAT YOU WANT TO SAY, AND NOT GIVING A DAMN." —ORSON WELLES

In grade school, I went door-to-door selling Camp Fire candy. After a few years I began to notice that the way I reacted as the person answered the door determined whether or not they bought a box of my almond caramel clusters (yum!) or mint patties.

Upon learning this trick—smile and be enthusiastic—I went on to become the top candy seller in Lawton, Oklahoma, and won the coveted forest green tent prize! Yes, I'm still proud.

Although this may seem trite and unrelated, I've kept this in mind as I took on various roles—paralegal, yoga teacher, therapist—as an adult. I'm a believer that you *do* catch more flies with honey, as they say. This month is about both style and beauty as the two are closely intertwined in how we view ourselves and present ourselves to the world.

When you hear style and/or beauty, what comes to mind? Take a moment to pen the answer in the margins or in your journal.

Is it Coco Chanel, New York Fashion Week, entertaining, home decor, Vogue magazine, Paris, a capsule wardrobe, kitten heels, beauty products, your grandmother, wholesome eating, an organized closet, etiquette?

According to Merriam-Webster, style is "a distinctive manner of expression or custom of behaving or conducting oneself" and beauty is "the quality or aggregate of qualities in a person or thing that gives pleasure to the senses or pleasurably exalts the mind or spirit."

While some may view style and beauty as vain or unimportant, I believe our outward appearances are a representation of our inner world and worthy of our attention. And this has little to do with our clothing or lipstick.

Let's do a little exploration around style. How would you describe yours—boho, artsy, glam, urban, edgy, understated, classic, casual, sporty? Consider how you've decorated your home and office, your favorite outfits, the music you listen to, the exhibits you like to see, how you enjoy spending your free time, your preferred mode of transportation, the makeup you wear (or don't wear), the way you talk and write, what you read, your temperament, and how you interact with others. All of these are manifestations of your personal style.

Do you feel like your answers to these questions are an accurate representation of your preferred signature style? If not, what would make them feel more authentic? Who are your style icons? What is it about them that you're drawn to? Sometimes it's the ease with which they run a meeting, their leopard-print office chaise lounge, the way they treat others, or their faux fur accents. Notice what it is about them and consider creating a collage or Pinterest board of what you believe connotes signature style.

Although beauty may be perceived as cosmetics or perfume to some, our inner beauty is reflected on the outside and self-compassion contributes to that glow. Speaking kindly and lovingly toward ourselves and showcasing a genuine, warm smile are two important ways we can share our beauty. If we don't feel good inside, it's hard to exude the radiance that makes someone beautiful and magnetic.

One of my VIA Strengths is Appreciation of Beauty (take the free quiz at viacharacter.org). I'm moved by music, art, and nature. This clearly has nothing to do with the cosmetic industry and everything to do with being sensitive and appreciating the beauty around me. When you think of beauty in your life, what comes to mind? Is it a vase of fresh-cut daffodils, a piece of art brought back from your travels, a brooch from your grandmother, a nail color, a nourishing skin cleanser?

We nurture our inner beauty through what we eat. For long-term support of inner beauty, consume nutrient-rich foods, greens, and healthy fats, rest to balance busyness with meditation, stay hydrated with tea and lemon water, and exercise. We'll explore this further in Wellness and Self-Care.

As the spring flowers push up from the soil and we begin to shed our layers, notice the beauty within and around you. Consider a trip to a botanical garden, a pedicure, a detox, a performing arts show, a revamp of your beauty routine, or a new shade of lipstick.

Beauty and style begin with self-love and come full circle with self-expression. As Coco said, "Adornment is never anything except a reflection of the heart."

Savvy Sources

BOOKS:
Lessons from Madame Chic by Jennifer Scott
Entre Nous by Debra Olivier
I Love Your Style by Amanda Brooks
Forever Chic by Tish Jett
Ooh La La by Jamie Cat Callan
Eat Pretty by Jolene Hart
The French Beauty Solution by Mathilde Thomas
Whole Beauty by Shiva Rose

APPS:
Cladwell
StyleBook

TRANQUILITY DU JOUR PODCASTS:
#42 Outer Beauty
#179 Signature Style
#259 Project 333
#289 Finding Your Ooh la la
#310 Style Secrets
#338 All About the Pretty
#351 At Home with Madame Chic
#354 The Good Karma Diet
#366 Polish Your Poise
#414 Parisian Charm School

notes:

COMPASSION IS THE NEW BLACK.

WEEK 1: STYLE & BEAUTY

Consider the persona you want to express to the world (we'll explore personal branding further in Entrepreneurship). You want your style to reflect your personality, but it also has to make sense in your field of work, your overall lifestyle, the city you live in, and align with your long-term goals (like overalls if you're craving country life). Set aside 30 minutes to play on Pinterest or to thumb through a few magazines.

Collage or create a stylebook using Pinterest. Consider accessories, social media, beloved causes, body language, entertaining, free time, décor, color, print, wardrobe staples, and texture. How are you most excited to showcase your signature style?

How can you infuse your days with more beauty? Think inner and outer beauty. Consider: nail care, smile, hydration, poetry, baking, skin care routine, forest bathing (bathe in nature with all your senses), moisturizer, creating a home sanctuary (flowers, candles, plants, light), performing arts, gardening, poetry, cooking, farmers' markets, perfume, snail mail, dance, positive mindset, slowing down, pillow spray, simple makeup.

Remember, our insides help our outsides shine. That's why we've focused on our dreams, love, and now inner and outer style and beauty. You radiate, I know you do!

weekly tranquility tools

- PLAN WEEK'S MITS
- PEN A LOVE NOTE
- SOAK IN THE TUB
- ARTIST DATE
- DIGITAL DAY OFF
- GREEN JUICE
- CLEAR CLUTTER
- BUY OR PICK FRESH FLOWERS

2
WEEK 2: CLOSET CLEARING

To create space for our signature style, let's shed what no longer resonates style-wise and do some spring cleaning by clearing out our closet (or cupboards or shelves)!

I know, I know, but I promise, this is a therapeutic step in our style journey. It's helpful to know what we have on hand. This process typically takes a few uninterrupted hours and, similar to a detox, will leave you feeling lighter!

Begin by pulling everything out of your closet (or cupboard or shelf). Next separate the items into assorted piles:

1. **KEEPERS.** These are your staples. Those items that fit, look good on you, match your lifestyle, and go with various pieces in your closet. Hang them back in your closet by color and category as you go. If it's cosmetics or cupboards you're cleaning out, same thing, put those staples back in their spot organizing by face, hair, and body.

2. **DONATE/SWAP.** Those pieces you once loved, thought you'd love, or simply don't fit you or your lifestyle anymore. Set these items aside. I love donating these items local charity thrift shop or hosting a clothing swap with friends.

3. **TRASH.** Set aside your damaged and past-their-prime pieces. Also those expired cosmetics.

4. **REPAIR/ALTER.** For those items that need a little TLC such as an alteration or button fix, create a separate pile.

5. **UNDECIDED.** Ah, these are the pieces you're just not sure about. Don't love them, don't hate them, but haven't worn in years. Toss these items aside if you're becoming overwhelmed. You can always come back to these items later with a fresh perspective.

Next, place those special occasion items like skiwear, beachwear, and formalwear toward the back of the closet unless you live near a resort or beach. It's good to have these pieces easily accessible, but not taking up the precious real estate of your staples.

Finally, toss your trash items, pass along your donate/swap items, fix your repair/alter items, and contemplate those undecided items. Now look at your keepers. Is there anything you'd like to add to them this season? Maybe an essential like a little black dress in your current size or a lavender accent scarf.

Note this and keep your eye out for the right item or accessory to bring your staples closer to your style board. No need to go on a big shopping spree. Sometimes it's a simple scarf in the season's color that brightens everything up!

weekly tranquility tools

- PLAN WEEK'S MITS
- PEN A LOVE NOTE
- SOAK IN THE TUB
- ARTIST DATE
- DIGITAL DAY OFF
- GREEN JUICE
- CLEAR CLUTTER
- BUY OR PICK FRESH FLOWERS

3 WEEK 3: HOME, OFFICE, TRAVEL

Let's consider our style at home, in the office, and while traveling. Similar to last week, creating a Pinterest board or collage to clarify your preferred style may be helpful.

AT HOME: How would you describe your home decor style? Boho, traditional, girly, artsy? Consider the colors, textures, and prints you're drawn to. Similar to your clothing, does your home decor reflect your current lifestyle? If not, consider a few shifts.

Look around each room with fresh eyes. Re-envision what you already have and move things around, paint, or reupholster. A few ways to spruce up on a budget include: add plants, a faux fur throw, or mirrors, hang twinkle lights, paint a wall in your favorite color, add lamps, add a signature rug like jute or leopard-print, pile on the pillows, add crown molding, try a new shower curtain, add fresh flowers.

IN THE OFFICE: You may have a big corner office, cubicle, desk spot that changes from day to day, home office, or anything in between. The key here is to have a space that serves as a productive respite during your work time. Similar to the home, greenery and fresh flowers (even one daffodil in a mason jar) add a bit of sunshine.

Curate a luxury toolkit (a bag, drawer, or nook) full of sensory delights: lip-gloss, essential oil, a scented candle, face wipes, mascara, slippers, a favorite mug, bags of tea, moisturizer, perfume oil, dark chocolate, Vitamin C drink packets, a book of poetry. Display a few framed photos or postcards; hang them on a wire or clip them to a ribbon. Fill a mug with your favorite pens. Frame inspiring quotes.

ON TRAVEL: When heading out for a weekend or week-long journey, do you have all the accoutrements to keep you comfortable and stylish? Being out of our routine and environment can lead to additional stressors, so it's helpful to pack lightly and carry creature comforts to help you feel your best.

I've found that the key to tranquil travel is layers, rolled clothing, and a rollaboard suitcase that fits in the overhead compartment. Many of the staples come with me in my carry-on: pain reliever, earplugs, headphones, healthy snacks, meds, lavender oil, journal, pen, books, laptop.

Consider your home, office, and travel style. What would help your current version feel aligned with or inspired by your ideal version? Similar to our personal style (and last week's mention of adding a scarf to spruce up the basics), it can often be as simple as making a small change to bring life into balance.

weekly tranquility tools

- **PLAN WEEK'S MITS**
- **PEN A LOVE NOTE**
- **SOAK IN THE TUB**
- **ARTIST DATE**
- **DIGITAL DAY OFF**
- **GREEN JUICE**
- **CLEAR CLUTTER**
- **BUY OR PICK FRESH FLOWERS**

WEAR BLACK, LIVE PINK.

WEEK 4: CAPSULE WARDROBE

A capsule wardrobe is a collection of essential and versatile pieces. The benefits of having a uniform (an outfit you wear regularly) or capsule wardrobe include: creating your signature look, no longer experiencing the "I have nothing to wear" dilemma, reducing decision fatigue, not buying frivolously, and having more time.

While there is no correct way to do this, I have some suggestions below on how you, too, can create yours with 10–40 pieces—whatever feels like a stretch and doable to you!

CREATE YOUR OWN:

1. After your closet clean out, count and assess your favorite 10–40 pieces. There's no magic number, choose what fits for you. Extras such as workout wear, intimates, sleepwear, coats/jackets, accessories, shoes, and special occasion pieces don't count in your total.
2. Create an inventory list of your chosen pieces and assign a number to each one. Set the other articles of clothing aside for now (or donate them).
3. Play dress up and snap photos of different ways to mix and match plus layer the items on your list. Print and post the photos inside your closet door or upload on an app (see Savvy Sources).
4. Note the combinations on your inventory sheet. Record the numbers and looks, such as two, six, and eight create a festive date night look. For an example, check out the layering of my uniform: the TranquiliT 2in1 fitted top and capri leggings at TranquiliT.com.

Here's an idea of a few wardrobe essentials: little black dress, black pants in a versatile fabric, black tank top, dark wash jeans, wrap dress, white tee, black blazer, cardigan, midi skirt.

Remember those accessories. They can turn your average black dress into a cocktail-worthy ensemble when paired with heels, a faux fur shrug, and sparkly earrings. Or a fancy black dress into a more casual chic look when paired with a denim shirt and sneakers.

Here are a few accessories to play with: warm smile, brooches, sunnies, scarves tied in the hair/around neck/around wrist/around handbag, necklaces (long faux pearls fancy up a black tee and jeans), earrings, hats, bags, arm/legwarmers, rings, umbrellas, belts, positive attitude, outerwear (faux fur, denim, trench coat, faux leather, parka, duster, peacoat, raincoat, cape), footwear (kitten heels, loafers, pumps, stilettos, wedges, mules, sandals, espadrilles, ballet flats, Mary Janes, ankle booties, tall boots, sneakers, clogs).

For a capsule wardrobe sample, check out TranquiliT's 11-piece capsule wardrobe and various ways to wear the items at TranquiliT.com/capsule. See p. 38 for more.

my capsule wardrobe

weekly tranquility tools

- PLAN WEEK'S MITS
- PEN A LOVE NOTE
- SOAK IN THE TUB
- ARTIST DATE
- DIGITAL DAY OFF
- GREEN JUICE
- CLEAR CLUTTER
- BUY OR PICK FRESH FLOWERS

seasonal life review

DATE: _____

SEASONALLY REFLECT ON AREAS OF YOUR LIFE. RATE EACH ONE WITH YOUR LEVEL OF SATISFACTION 10 = BLISS, 5 = SO-SO, 0 = BOO.

Here are some additional areas to consider: social life, romance, family, education, health, fitness, meaning, activism. Next, take a moment to note the areas that ranked low and create three action steps to increase your tranquility in these areas. Be gentle. Plant seeds. Watch dreams take root.

ACTION STEPS TO INCREASE AREAS THAT ARE LOWER THAN I'D LIKE:

seasonal checklist

- ○ WHEEL OF LIFE
- ○ DEEP CLEAN
- ○ PRACTICE ESSENTIALISM
- ○ TRY SOMETHING NEW
- ○ BED DAY
- ○ REARRANGE
- ○ GET CULTURED
- ○ TEND YOUR GARDEN
- ○ _____

monthly planner

MONTH: _____ **INTENTION:** _____

SUNDAY	MONDAY	TUESDAY	WEDNESDAY	THURSDAY	FRIDAY	SATURDAY

monthly tranquility tools and practices

- ○ CRAFT MONTH'S DREAMS
- ○ REVIEW BUDGET
- ○ WEEK 1
- ○ CREATE SOMETHING
- ○ READ TWO BOOKS
- ○ WEEK 2
- ○ VOLUNTEER
- ○ MANI/PEDI
- ○ WEEK 3
- ○ ENTERTAIN
- ○ MASSAGE
- ○ WEEK 4

month's dreams

month's review

moon phases

Notice your connection to the moon's cycles in these four phases: new, waxing, full, waning. Consider the prompts below as a way to tie into your Month's Dreams and provide space for monthly reflection.

new moon

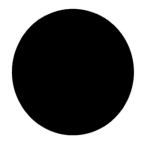

A TIME FOR SETTING INTENTIONS.
I WANT...

waxing moon

A TIME FOR ACTION.
I WILL...

full moon

A TIME FOR HARVEST AND CLOSURE.
I RELEASE...

waning moon

A TIME FOR SOFTENING.
I FEEL...

daily checklist

TRACK YOUR INCORPORATION OF THE DAILY TRANQUILITY TOOLS.

1

- MORNING ROUTINE
- DAILY DRESS-UP
- MINDFUL MOVEMENT
- EAT YOUR VEGGIES
- JOURNAL
- GOAL REVIEW
- GRATITUDE
- EVENING ROUTINE
- ____________

2

- MORNING ROUTINE
- DAILY DRESS-UP
- MINDFUL MOVEMENT
- EAT YOUR VEGGIES
- JOURNAL
- GOAL REVIEW
- GRATITUDE
- EVENING ROUTINE
- ____________

3

- MORNING ROUTINE
- DAILY DRESS-UP
- MINDFUL MOVEMENT
- EAT YOUR VEGGIES
- JOURNAL
- GOAL REVIEW
- GRATITUDE
- EVENING ROUTINE
- ____________

4

- MORNING ROUTINE
- DAILY DRESS-UP
- MINDFUL MOVEMENT
- EAT YOUR VEGGIES
- JOURNAL
- GOAL REVIEW
- GRATITUDE
- EVENING ROUTINE
- ____________

5

- MORNING ROUTINE
- DAILY DRESS-UP
- MINDFUL MOVEMENT
- EAT YOUR VEGGIES
- JOURNAL
- GOAL REVIEW
- GRATITUDE
- EVENING ROUTINE
- ____________

6

- MORNING ROUTINE
- DAILY DRESS-UP
- MINDFUL MOVEMENT
- EAT YOUR VEGGIES
- JOURNAL
- GOAL REVIEW
- GRATITUDE
- EVENING ROUTINE
- ____________

7

- MORNING ROUTINE
- DAILY DRESS-UP
- MINDFUL MOVEMENT
- EAT YOUR VEGGIES
- JOURNAL
- GOAL REVIEW
- GRATITUDE
- EVENING ROUTINE
- ____________

8

- MORNING ROUTINE
- DAILY DRESS-UP
- MINDFUL MOVEMENT
- EAT YOUR VEGGIES
- JOURNAL
- GOAL REVIEW
- GRATITUDE
- EVENING ROUTINE
- ____________

9

- MORNING ROUTINE
- DAILY DRESS-UP
- MINDFUL MOVEMENT
- EAT YOUR VEGGIES
- JOURNAL
- GOAL REVIEW
- GRATITUDE
- EVENING ROUTINE
- ____________

10

- MORNING ROUTINE
- DAILY DRESS-UP
- MINDFUL MOVEMENT
- EAT YOUR VEGGIES
- JOURNAL
- GOAL REVIEW
- GRATITUDE
- EVENING ROUTINE
- ____________

11

- MORNING ROUTINE
- DAILY DRESS-UP
- MINDFUL MOVEMENT
- EAT YOUR VEGGIES
- JOURNAL
- GOAL REVIEW
- GRATITUDE
- EVENING ROUTINE
- ____________

12

- MORNING ROUTINE
- DAILY DRESS-UP
- MINDFUL MOVEMENT
- EAT YOUR VEGGIES
- JOURNAL
- GOAL REVIEW
- GRATITUDE
- EVENING ROUTINE
- ____________

13

- MORNING ROUTINE
- DAILY DRESS-UP
- MINDFUL MOVEMENT
- EAT YOUR VEGGIES
- JOURNAL
- GOAL REVIEW
- GRATITUDE
- EVENING ROUTINE
- ____________

14

- MORNING ROUTINE
- DAILY DRESS-UP
- MINDFUL MOVEMENT
- EAT YOUR VEGGIES
- JOURNAL
- GOAL REVIEW
- GRATITUDE
- EVENING ROUTINE
- ____________

15

- MORNING ROUTINE
- DAILY DRESS-UP
- MINDFUL MOVEMENT
- EAT YOUR VEGGIES
- JOURNAL
- GOAL REVIEW
- GRATITUDE
- EVENING ROUTINE
- ____________

16

- MORNING ROUTINE
- DAILY DRESS-UP
- MINDFUL MOVEMENT
- EAT YOUR VEGGIES
- JOURNAL
- GOAL REVIEW
- GRATITUDE
- EVENING ROUTINE
- ____________

17

- MORNING ROUTINE
- DAILY DRESS-UP
- MINDFUL MOVEMENT
- EAT YOUR VEGGIES
- JOURNAL
- GOAL REVIEW
- GRATITUDE
- EVENING ROUTINE
- ____________

18

- MORNING ROUTINE
- DAILY DRESS-UP
- MINDFUL MOVEMENT
- EAT YOUR VEGGIES
- JOURNAL
- GOAL REVIEW
- GRATITUDE
- EVENING ROUTINE
- ____________

19

- MORNING ROUTINE
- DAILY DRESS-UP
- MINDFUL MOVEMENT
- EAT YOUR VEGGIES
- JOURNAL
- GOAL REVIEW
- GRATITUDE
- EVENING ROUTINE
- ____________

20

- MORNING ROUTINE
- DAILY DRESS-UP
- MINDFUL MOVEMENT
- EAT YOUR VEGGIES
- JOURNAL
- GOAL REVIEW
- GRATITUDE
- EVENING ROUTINE
- ____________

21

- MORNING ROUTINE
- DAILY DRESS-UP
- MINDFUL MOVEMENT
- EAT YOUR VEGGIES
- JOURNAL
- GOAL REVIEW
- GRATITUDE
- EVENING ROUTINE
- ____________

22

- MORNING ROUTINE
- DAILY DRESS-UP
- MINDFUL MOVEMENT
- EAT YOUR VEGGIES
- JOURNAL
- GOAL REVIEW
- GRATITUDE
- EVENING ROUTINE
- ____________

23

- MORNING ROUTINE
- DAILY DRESS-UP
- MINDFUL MOVEMENT
- EAT YOUR VEGGIES
- JOURNAL
- GOAL REVIEW
- GRATITUDE
- EVENING ROUTINE
- ____________

24

- MORNING ROUTINE
- DAILY DRESS-UP
- MINDFUL MOVEMENT
- EAT YOUR VEGGIES
- JOURNAL
- GOAL REVIEW
- GRATITUDE
- EVENING ROUTINE
- ____________

25

- MORNING ROUTINE
- DAILY DRESS-UP
- MINDFUL MOVEMENT
- EAT YOUR VEGGIES
- JOURNAL
- GOAL REVIEW
- GRATITUDE
- EVENING ROUTINE
- ____________

26

- MORNING ROUTINE
- DAILY DRESS-UP
- MINDFUL MOVEMENT
- EAT YOUR VEGGIES
- JOURNAL
- GOAL REVIEW
- GRATITUDE
- EVENING ROUTINE
- ____________

27

- MORNING ROUTINE
- DAILY DRESS-UP
- MINDFUL MOVEMENT
- EAT YOUR VEGGIES
- JOURNAL
- GOAL REVIEW
- GRATITUDE
- EVENING ROUTINE
- ____________

28

- MORNING ROUTINE
- DAILY DRESS-UP
- MINDFUL MOVEMENT
- EAT YOUR VEGGIES
- JOURNAL
- GOAL REVIEW
- GRATITUDE
- EVENING ROUTINE
- ____________

29

- MORNING ROUTINE
- DAILY DRESS-UP
- MINDFUL MOVEMENT
- EAT YOUR VEGGIES
- JOURNAL
- GOAL REVIEW
- GRATITUDE
- EVENING ROUTINE
- ____________

30

- MORNING ROUTINE
- DAILY DRESS-UP
- MINDFUL MOVEMENT
- EAT YOUR VEGGIES
- JOURNAL
- GOAL REVIEW
- GRATITUDE
- EVENING ROUTINE
- ____________

creativity

"EVERYBODY IS TALENTED BECAUSE EVERYBODY WHO IS HUMAN HAS SOMETHING TO EXPRESS."
—BRENDA UELAND

When I first picked up Julia Cameron's *The Artist's Way*, I'd just completed my first yoga teacher training. I was in my mid-20s, restless, and seeking a life trajectory that didn't involve my traditional 9-to-5.

The book is touted as "a course in discovering and recovering your creative self," a 12-step program similarly aligned to the structure of Alcoholics Anonymous. As someone who struggled to draw stick figures and made birds out of the letter "m," considering myself an artist felt far-fetched, but I was willing to give it a go.

My teacher training friend, Susan, agreed to join me on the 12-week adventure as a sort of accountability buddy. We met at a café to talk through our plans—both eager to see what this book would bring. It received praise from so many people I met during this time of soul searching that I felt there had to be nuggets inside to help me make sense of adulting.

Although Susan dropped the program after week one when she realized she couldn't create the space for it, I continued, hungry for a sense of purpose. Within a few weeks, there seemed to be some traction. I began to see things in a new light. I questioned my beliefs about creativity and developed a new sense of hope. I saw that life could be different, more meaningful.

I did my Morning Pages (three pages written longhand each morning), took my Artist Dates (a solo jaunt to nurture your creativity), and worked through the exercises at the end of each chapter. I considered what I loved as a child, what imaginary lives I craved, what kept me stuck, and what boundaries needed to be set.

Once I got to the exercises in week eight, I started to envision a tiny yoga studio space in the living room of my fourth floor walk-up. I wrote on a Post-it note the basic supplies I'd need: yoga mats, blankets, screens to block the view of my kitchen and bedroom, eye pillows, tea cups, thermos for chai, notebook for sign-ins.

As I reviewed this list, I realized how few supplies were necessary to launch the venture. This was the nudge I needed to begin the move away from that 9–5 and into a world of my own. Within one month, I was inviting strangers into my living room to do yoga.

That was 20 years ago, and I've been on a mission to live and teach creativity ever since. Considering I didn't view myself as an artist—I thought that was for the Monets of the world—and was traumatized by my lack of talent in those early art classes, I've spent years peeling away the layers of that story and those experiences.

Dictionary.com defines creativity as "the ability to transcend traditional ideas, rules, patterns, relationships, or the like, and to create meaningful new ideas, forms, methods, interpretations, etc.; originality, progressiveness, or imagination."

So you see, we're all artists. Yes, YOU! We create every single day—meals, outfits, stories, routes to work, plans, ideas, dreams, desires, experiences. Each day is a fresh canvas for us to paint in tiny, controlled dots or in bold pastel strokes.

Consider what moves you and what you loved as a child. Look for creative opportunities. Spend time in nature. Do things differently. Take a hand lettering class and brush letter your thank-you note envelopes. Go to an exhibit. Sit outside at a café to sip tea and flip through a magazine filled with inspiring images. Browse a bookstore. Study with artists you admire. Try an online tutorial.

This month we'll be exploring types of creativity, ways to express creativity (even if your birds are the letter "m"), and various practices to fuel our creativity.

Let creativity infuse your days, for as Annie Dillard reminds us, "How we spend our days is how we spend our lives."

Savvy Sources

BOOKS:
The Artist's Way by Julia Cameron
The 12 Secrets of Highly Creative Women by Gail McMeekin
Big Magic by Elizabeth Gilbert
The Creative Habit by Twyla Tharp
Steal Like an Artist by Austin Kleon
The War of Art by Steven Pressfield
Creative Revolution by Flora Bowley
Cultivating the Creative Life by Alena Hennessy

APPS:
Brainsparker Creativity Cards
Art Set
Penultimate

TRANQUILITY DU JOUR PODCASTS:
#78 Creativity Cravings
#122 Being Succulent with SARK
#152 Musings on Creativity
#154 Guide to Creativity
#184 Creative Awakenings
#238 Abundant Wild Life
#242 Brave Intuitive Painting
#273 Making Your Creative Mark
#307 Yoga + Creativity
#373 Creative Practice

notes:

BOOKEND THE DAY WITH REFLECTION AND INTENTION.

1

WEEK 1: ARTIST DATES

Julia Cameron defines an Artist Date as a "once-weekly, festive, solo expedition to explore something that interests you. The Artist Date need not be overtly 'artistic'—think mischief more than mastery. Artist Dates fire up the imagination. They spark whimsy. They encourage play. Since art is about the play of ideas, they feed our creative work by replenishing our inner well of images and inspiration. When choosing an Artist Date, ask yourself, 'what sounds fun?'—and then allow yourself to try it."

Here's an assortment of Artist Date ideas: visit a farmers' market, go to your local library, create a kitchen herb garden, write in your journal at a sidewalk café, visit a craft shop, pick up something new to play with (paint, stamps, paper, pens, washi tape), collage, set up your creative space at home, visit a museum, head to the countryside, play visitor in your city, play on Pinterest, make a playlist, watch a foreign film, go window shopping, go thrift shopping, visit a flea market, browse a bookstore, spend time in the magazine section, visit a local park, people watch, snap photos along the way, explore a new neighborhood, go for a bike ride, make a new recipe, read poetry outside, pick up an adult coloring book and break out the colored pencils, make an inspiration board that is filled with images that make you smile, play with paint, take a yoga class, take a dance class, take an online class, attend a workshop, take up hand lettering, visit a cemetery, try a new type of tea, walk through a street fair, visit the nearest garden in bloom, visit an art gallery, get a tarot card reading, attend a live music event, design a spring-focused vision board, fly a kite, visit an animal sanctuary, or sit outside and meditate.

Make a list of Artist Date options that resonate and schedule them in your planner.

weekly tranquility tools

- ○ PLAN WEEK'S MITS
- ○ PEN A LOVE NOTE
- ○ SOAK IN THE TUB
- ○ ARTIST DATE
- ○ DIGITAL DAY OFF
- ○ GREEN JUICE
- ○ CLEAR CLUTTER
- ○ BUY OR PICK FRESH FLOWERS

WEEK 2: ART JOURNAL

Art journaling (also known as sketchbooking and visual journaling) is the creative process of combining color, words, and images onto a page. This is a fun practice done solo or with a group of friends. No prior experience is needed, so it's great for beginners. Consider making an event out of it: invite a few people over, serve treats (recipes p. 37) and drinks, play inspiring music, share supplies, spread materials out on the floor or table, experience the magic of creating, host a show and tell at the end.

It differs from scrapbooking in that it's about the process, not the outcome AND about ideas, not just memories. And the best part? It's good for you. According to an article by Cathy Malchiodi in *Psychology Today*, studies show that regular art journaling increases the flow of serotonin to the brain and increases the number of immune cells flowing through the body. Let's get started!

1. Gather your art journaling tools: a journal*, black Sharpie or permanent black artist pen, glue stick, ephemera (bits of paper with words and/or images from magazines, etc.). Optional: acrylic or watercolor paint, paintbrushes (or use an expired credit card to paint), paper towels, colored pencils, pencil, washi tape, scissors, stamps, stamp pads, wax paper (to place between freshly painted pages as they dry).

2. Make a background with paint, with a big image, by rubbing a stamp pad over it, or with colored pencils to avoid starting on a blank page.

3. Add images and words from your ephemera into a collage aligned with a theme that resonates.

4. Add words by writing over the images.

*Choose spiral or sewn binding and any size: 3.5 x 5 to 8.5 x 11, A3 to A7, or B5 to B7.

IDEAS:

- Make art out of your favorite quote, poem, or lyrics
- Create lists
- Write out your feelings and cover the words with paint
- Create collages using words and images from magazines
- Design a themed page such as self-care, style, and dreams
- Create a page using only images with your favorite color
- Doodle and fill in the doodles with paint

Gather your supplies and design a page that represents creativity to you. Remember, this is all about letting your creative spark emerge. There's no right way or wrong way to do this. Promise!

weekly tranquility tools

- ○ PLAN WEEK'S MITS
- ○ SOAK IN THE TUB
- ○ DIGITAL DAY OFF
- ○ CLEAR CLUTTER
- ○ PEN A LOVE NOTE
- ○ ARTIST DATE
- ○ GREEN JUICE
- ○ BUY OR PICK FRESH FLOWERS

WEEK 3: CREATIVE EXPRESSION

Consider these four questions:
1. What do you think of when you hear the word creativity?
2. Who embodies creativity to you? Why?
3. What are ways you express creativity?
4. How else would you like to express creativity?

Note your answer to number four and consider if there's anything else you'd like to add. Choose one creative practice (e.g., brush hand lettering, knitting, sketching, art journaling, writing, photography, music, making jewelry or bath products, cooking, dancing, poetry, improv, theater, macramé, origami, gardening, scrapbooking, woodworking, embroidery) and take one micromovement toward it this week.

It can be new to you or a practice you'd like to deepen.

For example, if you chose brush hand lettering, look for online tutorials and set aside one hour to practice. Or look for in-person workshops and sign up.

If you chose dancing, look for nearby drop-in classes and sign up. Turn on some fun tunes and dance at home. Or review dance tutorial videos online and practice your moves.

The idea is to move that creative expression off your wish list and into reality. You've got this!

weekly tranquility tools

- ○ PLAN WEEK'S MITS
- ○ SOAK IN THE TUB
- ○ DIGITAL DAY OFF
- ○ CLEAR CLUTTER
- ○ PEN A LOVE NOTE
- ○ ARTIST DATE
- ○ GREEN JUICE
- ○ BUY OR PICK FRESH FLOWERS

4 WEEK 4: LIVING YOUR ART

Many daily decisions offer the opportunity to express our creative spark—from what we eat, to what we wear, to how we communicate, to how we spend our free time, to what we write with and on, to what we read, to how we set up our space. Below you'll find a smattering of ideas to bring more creativity into our day through small, simple shifts.

Try a new type of tea. Listen to a new podcast (you know about *Tranquility du Jour*, right?!). Add a new vocabulary word to your mix. Try socks with your sandals. Add a striped paper straw or reusable straw (never plastic) to your favorite libation. Take notes with a Crayola marker. Bring an artsy notebook or pink legal pad to your next meeting. Add a few drops of essential oil to your bath. Bring fresh-cut tulips into your home or office. Tote your morning smoothie to work in a Mason jar. Refill with water and reuse throughout the day to stay hydrated. Stop into that thrift store or bookstore you always pass on your way home from work to simply browse. Insert a tea bag in your next thank-you note and seal it with washi tape.

Tuck a book you've been meaning to read inside your bag and find pockets of space to pull it out while waiting in lines, at appointments, or for your barista to make your beverage. Try a new yoga, dance, or meditation teacher. Set up your creative space at home with soothing colors schemes, a Mason jar filled with markers and washi tape, meaningful mementos, journals, writing tools, and art supplies. Light a candle. Plug in twinkle lights. Listen to a new genre of music. Look for ways to add more whole foods to your meal planning. Create a meal plan to combat getting hangry and making less-than-ideal choices.

Add a chunky necklace to your ensemble. Set your writing tools out on your desk in a teacup with an inspiring message. Move your furniture around, add a brightly colored throw, and toss your magazines into a wicker basket. Try a new perfume. Frame art postcards and display in your workspace. Tie ribbons around pussy willows. Weed your garden (literally and figuratively). Use your good china. Wear a flower in your hair.

Take note of a few ideas that resonate with you and try them out this week. You ARE creative and life provides the opportunity to showcase it every single day. This week dabble with a few of these ideas to add more creativity into your every day. As Thoreau said, "The world is but a canvas to the imagination."

weekly tranquility tools

- ○ PLAN WEEK'S MITS
- ○ PEN A LOVE NOTE
- ○ SOAK IN THE TUB
- ○ ARTIST DATE
- ○ DIGITAL DAY OFF
- ○ GREEN JUICE
- ○ CLEAR CLUTTER
- ○ BUY OR PICK FRESH FLOWERS

everyday creativity

LOOK FOR BEAUTY on your DAILY walk and SNAP A PHOTO. tuck a LOVE NOTE inside your PARTNER or child's bag. TRY A NEW RECIPE. pick up an herb, fruit, or vegetable that's NEW to you and CREATE A DISH using it. drive a NEW ROUTE TO WORK. start your day differently than usual—incorporate movement or MEDITATION. wear a new shade of LIPSTICK. add a scarf in a VIBRANT color. WANDER DURING YOUR LUNCH BREAK. picnic in the PARK. try a new type of tea. LISTEN to a new podcast. add a new VOCABULARY WORD to your mix. add a STRIPED PAPER STRAW to your favorite LIBATION. take notes with a CRAYOLA MAKER. bring an artsy notebook or PINK LEGAL PAD to your next meeting. add a few drops of LAVENDER OIL to your bath. tote your MORNING SMOOTHIE to work in a MASON JAR. bring FRESH-CUT FLOWERS to your home or office. browse a THRIFT STORE or bookstore. tuck a TEA BAG inside and seal your next THANK-YOU NOTE with WASHI tape. try a new YOGA, DANCE, or meditation TEACHER. light a candle. plug in TWINKLE LIGHTS. listen to a NEW GENRE of music. look for ways to add more WHOLE FOODS. create a meal plan. add a CHUNKY NECKLACE to your ensemble. set your WRITING TOOLS on your desk in a VINTAGE tea cup. MOVE YOUR FURNITURE AROUND, add a brightly-colored THROW, and toss your magazines into a WICKER BASKET. try a new perfume. display POSTCARDS from art exhibits in frames. WEED YOUR GARDEN (literally and figuratively). WEAR A FLOWER IN YOUR HAIR.

monthly planner

MONTH: _____   INTENTION: _____

SUNDAY	MONDAY	TUESDAY	WEDNESDAY	THURSDAY	FRIDAY	SATURDAY

monthly tranquility tools and practices

- ○ CRAFT MONTH'S DREAMS
- ○ REVIEW BUDGET
- ○ WEEK 1

- ○ CREATE SOMETHING
- ○ READ TWO BOOKS
- ○ WEEK 2

- ○ VOLUNTEER
- ○ MANI/PEDI
- ○ WEEK 3

- ○ ENTERTAIN
- ○ MASSAGE
- ○ WEEK 4

month's dreams

DOODLE, LIST, COLLAGE, OR WRITE WHAT YOU'D LIKE TO MANIFEST THIS MONTH.

month's review

REVISIT YOUR MONTH'S DREAMS AND NOTE HOW THEY UNFOLDED FOR YOU.

moon phases

Notice your connection to the moon's cycles in these four phases: new, waxing, full, waning. Consider the prompts below as a way to tie into your Month's Dreams and provide space for monthly reflection.

new moon

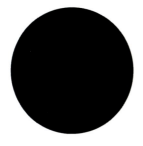

A TIME FOR SETTING INTENTIONS.
I WANT . . .

waxing moon

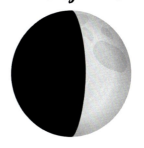

A TIME FOR ACTION.
I WILL . . .

full moon

A TIME FOR HARVEST AND CLOSURE.
I RELEASE . . .

waning moon

A TIME FOR SOFTENING.
I FEEL . . .

daily checklist

TRACK YOUR INCORPORATION OF THE DAILY TRANQUILITY TOOLS.

1
- ○ MORNING ROUTINE
- ○ DAILY DRESS-UP
- ○ MINDFUL MOVEMENT
- ○ EAT YOUR VEGGIES
- ○ JOURNAL
- ○ GOAL REVIEW
- ○ GRATITUDE
- ○ EVENING ROUTINE
- ○ ______________

2
- ○ MORNING ROUTINE
- ○ DAILY DRESS-UP
- ○ MINDFUL MOVEMENT
- ○ EAT YOUR VEGGIES
- ○ JOURNAL
- ○ GOAL REVIEW
- ○ GRATITUDE
- ○ EVENING ROUTINE
- ○ ______________

3
- ○ MORNING ROUTINE
- ○ DAILY DRESS-UP
- ○ MINDFUL MOVEMENT
- ○ EAT YOUR VEGGIES
- ○ JOURNAL
- ○ GOAL REVIEW
- ○ GRATITUDE
- ○ EVENING ROUTINE
- ○ ______________

4
- ○ MORNING ROUTINE
- ○ DAILY DRESS-UP
- ○ MINDFUL MOVEMENT
- ○ EAT YOUR VEGGIES
- ○ JOURNAL
- ○ GOAL REVIEW
- ○ GRATITUDE
- ○ EVENING ROUTINE
- ○ ______________

5
- ○ MORNING ROUTINE
- ○ DAILY DRESS-UP
- ○ MINDFUL MOVEMENT
- ○ EAT YOUR VEGGIES
- ○ JOURNAL
- ○ GOAL REVIEW
- ○ GRATITUDE
- ○ EVENING ROUTINE
- ○ ______________

6
- ○ MORNING ROUTINE
- ○ DAILY DRESS-UP
- ○ MINDFUL MOVEMENT
- ○ EAT YOUR VEGGIES
- ○ JOURNAL
- ○ GOAL REVIEW
- ○ GRATITUDE
- ○ EVENING ROUTINE
- ○ ______________

7
- ○ MORNING ROUTINE
- ○ DAILY DRESS-UP
- ○ MINDFUL MOVEMENT
- ○ EAT YOUR VEGGIES
- ○ JOURNAL
- ○ GOAL REVIEW
- ○ GRATITUDE
- ○ EVENING ROUTINE
- ○ ______________

8
- ○ MORNING ROUTINE
- ○ DAILY DRESS-UP
- ○ MINDFUL MOVEMENT
- ○ EAT YOUR VEGGIES
- ○ JOURNAL
- ○ GOAL REVIEW
- ○ GRATITUDE
- ○ EVENING ROUTINE
- ○ ______________

9
- ○ MORNING ROUTINE
- ○ DAILY DRESS-UP
- ○ MINDFUL MOVEMENT
- ○ EAT YOUR VEGGIES
- ○ JOURNAL
- ○ GOAL REVIEW
- ○ GRATITUDE
- ○ EVENING ROUTINE
- ○ ______________

10
- ○ MORNING ROUTINE
- ○ DAILY DRESS-UP
- ○ MINDFUL MOVEMENT
- ○ EAT YOUR VEGGIES
- ○ JOURNAL
- ○ GOAL REVIEW
- ○ GRATITUDE
- ○ EVENING ROUTINE
- ○ ______________

11
- ○ MORNING ROUTINE
- ○ DAILY DRESS-UP
- ○ MINDFUL MOVEMENT
- ○ EAT YOUR VEGGIES
- ○ JOURNAL
- ○ GOAL REVIEW
- ○ GRATITUDE
- ○ EVENING ROUTINE
- ○ ______________

12
- ○ MORNING ROUTINE
- ○ DAILY DRESS-UP
- ○ MINDFUL MOVEMENT
- ○ EAT YOUR VEGGIES
- ○ JOURNAL
- ○ GOAL REVIEW
- ○ GRATITUDE
- ○ EVENING ROUTINE
- ○ ______________

13
- ○ MORNING ROUTINE
- ○ DAILY DRESS-UP
- ○ MINDFUL MOVEMENT
- ○ EAT YOUR VEGGIES
- ○ JOURNAL
- ○ GOAL REVIEW
- ○ GRATITUDE
- ○ EVENING ROUTINE
- ○ ______________

14
- ○ MORNING ROUTINE
- ○ DAILY DRESS-UP
- ○ MINDFUL MOVEMENT
- ○ EAT YOUR VEGGIES
- ○ JOURNAL
- ○ GOAL REVIEW
- ○ GRATITUDE
- ○ EVENING ROUTINE
- ○ ______________

15
- ○ MORNING ROUTINE
- ○ DAILY DRESS-UP
- ○ MINDFUL MOVEMENT
- ○ EAT YOUR VEGGIES
- ○ JOURNAL
- ○ GOAL REVIEW
- ○ GRATITUDE
- ○ EVENING ROUTINE
- ○ ______________

16
- ○ MORNING ROUTINE
- ○ DAILY DRESS-UP
- ○ MINDFUL MOVEMENT
- ○ EAT YOUR VEGGIES
- ○ JOURNAL
- ○ GOAL REVIEW
- ○ GRATITUDE
- ○ EVENING ROUTINE
- ○ ______________

17
- ○ MORNING ROUTINE
- ○ DAILY DRESS-UP
- ○ MINDFUL MOVEMENT
- ○ EAT YOUR VEGGIES
- ○ JOURNAL
- ○ GOAL REVIEW
- ○ GRATITUDE
- ○ EVENING ROUTINE
- ○ ______________

18
- ○ MORNING ROUTINE
- ○ DAILY DRESS-UP
- ○ MINDFUL MOVEMENT
- ○ EAT YOUR VEGGIES
- ○ JOURNAL
- ○ GOAL REVIEW
- ○ GRATITUDE
- ○ EVENING ROUTINE
- ○ ______________

19
- ○ MORNING ROUTINE
- ○ DAILY DRESS-UP
- ○ MINDFUL MOVEMENT
- ○ EAT YOUR VEGGIES
- ○ JOURNAL
- ○ GOAL REVIEW
- ○ GRATITUDE
- ○ EVENING ROUTINE
- ○ ______________

20
- ○ MORNING ROUTINE
- ○ DAILY DRESS-UP
- ○ MINDFUL MOVEMENT
- ○ EAT YOUR VEGGIES
- ○ JOURNAL
- ○ GOAL REVIEW
- ○ GRATITUDE
- ○ EVENING ROUTINE
- ○ ______________

21
- ○ MORNING ROUTINE
- ○ DAILY DRESS-UP
- ○ MINDFUL MOVEMENT
- ○ EAT YOUR VEGGIES
- ○ JOURNAL
- ○ GOAL REVIEW
- ○ GRATITUDE
- ○ EVENING ROUTINE
- ○ ______________

22
- ○ MORNING ROUTINE
- ○ DAILY DRESS-UP
- ○ MINDFUL MOVEMENT
- ○ EAT YOUR VEGGIES
- ○ JOURNAL
- ○ GOAL REVIEW
- ○ GRATITUDE
- ○ EVENING ROUTINE
- ○ ______________

23
- ○ MORNING ROUTINE
- ○ DAILY DRESS-UP
- ○ MINDFUL MOVEMENT
- ○ EAT YOUR VEGGIES
- ○ JOURNAL
- ○ GOAL REVIEW
- ○ GRATITUDE
- ○ EVENING ROUTINE
- ○ ______________

24
- ○ MORNING ROUTINE
- ○ DAILY DRESS-UP
- ○ MINDFUL MOVEMENT
- ○ EAT YOUR VEGGIES
- ○ JOURNAL
- ○ GOAL REVIEW
- ○ GRATITUDE
- ○ EVENING ROUTINE
- ○ ______________

25
- ○ MORNING ROUTINE
- ○ DAILY DRESS-UP
- ○ MINDFUL MOVEMENT
- ○ EAT YOUR VEGGIES
- ○ JOURNAL
- ○ GOAL REVIEW
- ○ GRATITUDE
- ○ EVENING ROUTINE
- ○ ______________

26
- ○ MORNING ROUTINE
- ○ DAILY DRESS-UP
- ○ MINDFUL MOVEMENT
- ○ EAT YOUR VEGGIES
- ○ JOURNAL
- ○ GOAL REVIEW
- ○ GRATITUDE
- ○ EVENING ROUTINE
- ○ ______________

27
- ○ MORNING ROUTINE
- ○ DAILY DRESS-UP
- ○ MINDFUL MOVEMENT
- ○ EAT YOUR VEGGIES
- ○ JOURNAL
- ○ GOAL REVIEW
- ○ GRATITUDE
- ○ EVENING ROUTINE
- ○ ______________

28
- ○ MORNING ROUTINE
- ○ DAILY DRESS-UP
- ○ MINDFUL MOVEMENT
- ○ EAT YOUR VEGGIES
- ○ JOURNAL
- ○ GOAL REVIEW
- ○ GRATITUDE
- ○ EVENING ROUTINE
- ○ ______________

29
- ○ MORNING ROUTINE
- ○ DAILY DRESS-UP
- ○ MINDFUL MOVEMENT
- ○ EAT YOUR VEGGIES
- ○ JOURNAL
- ○ GOAL REVIEW
- ○ GRATITUDE
- ○ EVENING ROUTINE
- ○ ______________

30
- ○ MORNING ROUTINE
- ○ DAILY DRESS-UP
- ○ MINDFUL MOVEMENT
- ○ EAT YOUR VEGGIES
- ○ JOURNAL
- ○ GOAL REVIEW
- ○ GRATITUDE
- ○ EVENING ROUTINE
- ○ ______________

minimalism

"CLEARING CLUTTER—BE IT PHYSICAL, MENTAL, EMOTIONAL, OR SPIRITUAL—BRINGS ABOUT EASE AND INSPIRES A SENSE OF PEACE, CALM, AND TRANQUILITY."
—LAURIE BUCHANAN

I grew up in a modest home overflowing with books (of course I blame my parents for being a bibliophile), hobby-related items such as cameras, fabric paints, yarn, sewing machines, and family heirlooms.

Below is a story of how my desire to accumulate and do more grew over time into unhealthy habits until a wake-up call in 2012.

Mom and I spent my spring breaks through junior high and high school heading to visit her childhood friend in San Antonio and hitting the malls. Everything truly IS bigger in Texas, especially their shopping!

I'd save my $2 weekly allowance from cleaning at home and from my part-time department store job all year just for this week. I'd also sell lots of my clothing at second-hand shops to make money to buy more clothing. Oh, the irony. Toting around shopping bags and opening new items from the tissue paper-wrapped packages was quite the thrill.

When I set up my first apartments in Colorado, Old Town Alexandria (outside of Washington, DC), and in DC, I found beautiful things at thrift shops to furnish my tiny homes.

For years I loved stopping into second-hand shops and coming out with a new skirt or top, browsing bookstores in hope of finding a quick fix, and heading into "Tarjay" for kitty litter and coming out with a cartful of trinkets.

Moving my yoga studios into larger spaces over 18 years meant I was always on the prowl for inventory and furnishings. Accumulating and restocking became the norm.

Exposed to art journaling on a creativity retreat in 2010 with Lisa Sonora Beam, I began acquiring art supplies and saving materials that might work as ephemera in a future art journal spread.

During this phase, I also fell in love with vintage and boho style, so I'd scour Etsy, thrift stores, and second-hand shops to add pieces to my wardrobe and sell at the studios and through TranquiliT.com's own vintage/reclaimed page. I had vintage dresses hanging from curtain rods, crinolines hanging from my bookshelves, and numerous vintage purses set out on display in my very small space.

In 2012, my beloved Gramma passed away and I went through a deep state of mourning. She'd been a constant in my life since early childhood and we had a deep connection. Losing her shook my world and the grief led to reflecting on what really mattered.

Later that year while leading retreats in France, I read Francine Jay's *The Joy of Less: A Minimalist Living Guide* and came across a New York Times article called "The Busy Trap." My views on accumulating stuff and being busy began to change. I stopped declaring myself crazy busy.

Toward the end of the book Jay writes, "With minimalist living comes freedom—freedom from debt, from clutter, and from the rat race. Each extraneous thing eliminated from your life—be it an unused item, unnecessary purchase, or unfulfilling task—feels like a weight lifted from your shoulders. You'll have fewer errands to run and less to shop for, pay for, clean, maintain, and insure."

She goes on, "The same thing happens when our lives are too full— of commitments, of clutter, and of nonessential stuff. We don't have 'room' for new experiences, and miss out on chances to develop ourselves and deepen our relationships. Being minimalists helps us remedy this. By purging the excess from our homes, our schedules, and our minds, we empty our cups—giving us infinite capacity for life, love, hopes, dreams, and copious amounts of joy."

Having a life too full really resonated with me. For years I'd added more to my plate—things, commitments, to-dos—and I felt the weight. After reading this book, losing my Gramma, and doing some soul searching, I removed myself from day-to-day operations of my two yoga studios. I stopped going to Targét for fun. I took down the vintage items on display in my home and donated them. I stopped selling vintage and reclaimed items on Etsy and TranquiliT. And, I gave away many items stored in my closet—clothing, a leopard-print rug, a chandelier, and two sewing machines.

While I still have a book-buying problem, I've returned to Kindle to lessen the influx of books and have been surrendering many to Goodwill and friends. And I still enjoy a romp through a department store, although it's now limited to once or twice a year. I walk right past most vintage and thrift shops to avoid the temptation. I sold my two studios to free up time, energy, money, and space. Each year I do a few home purges and reorganize during the process. Unwanted items are passed along to a new, loving caretaker.

To lessen my waste, I skip plastic straws, utensils, and bags. Instead, I tote a fork, cloth napkin, a metal straw in my handbag and bring a reusable bag to the store. I'm less trigger-happy to purchase things online. Instead, I try to focus on experiences and items that will enhance my lifestyle such as theatre tickets or a bouquet of cut flowers. I also set up a mint.com account to track my spending habits (way too much on candles) and budgets.

Although I'm far from perfect, I'm working toward living a more minimalist lifestyle through these small daily actions coupled with bigger shifts such as letting go of a business I created 18 years ago. There is so much more to be done, but similar to our year's dreams, I like to think of it as one tiny micromovement at a time.

So what is minimalism you may wonder? According to Danny Dover, author of *The Minimalist Mindset*, "Minimalism is the constant art of editing your life." The Minimalists write that, "At its core, minimalism is the intentional promotion of the things we most value and the removal of everything that distracts us from it. It is a life that forces intentionality. And as a result, it forces improvements in almost all aspects of your life."

I think of minimalism as the practice of shedding what isn't essential to focus my time, energy, and money on what IS. For me, that's relationships, experiences, saving animals, creating, and well-being. When my time and attention aren't focused on these things, I feel myself shriveling like a sad little prune. When I do focus on these things, I'm plump and alive.

As author Joshua Becker reminds us, "Sometimes, minimizing possessions means a dream must die. But this is not always a bad thing. Sometimes, it takes giving up the person we wanted to be in order to fully appreciate the person we can actually become." Here's to who we are becoming and living in alignment with our values. One release at a time.

Savvy Sources

BOOKS:
You Can Buy Happiness (and It's Cheap) by Tammy Strobel
The Year of Less by Cait Flanders
The Joy of Less by Francine Jay
*Give a Sh*t* by Ashlee Piper
The Life-Changing Magic of Tidying Up by Marie Kondo
L'art de la Simplicité by Dominique Loreau

APPS:
MinimaList
Unroll.Me

TRANQUILITY DU JOUR PODCASTS:
#149 Secrets of Simplicity
#207 Simplification
#253 You Can Buy Happiness
#259 Simplicity
#389 Less = More
#426 Breaking Up With Busy
#438 Living The Simply Luxurious Life

notes:

1 WEEK 1: QUESTIONS

This week we're diving into minimalism by exploring the minimalist philosophy and asking ourselves some BIG questions. Let's get started with reflection.

1. What would living with more simplicity look like to you? What daily habits would help you live more simply?
2. What would you like to add to your life? Subtract?
3. List all of your current commitments and prioritize them in order of most essential to least essential. Consider eliminating a few of your least essential commitments.
4. Look around at all of your stuff. Note how much of it you've used in the past three months. What can you let go of?
5. Track your spending and time usage this week. Does it align with what is most important to you? Use the time tracker on p. 32 and the weekly spending on p. 41.

Explore these questions and note anything surprising, enlightening, or challenging (or anything in between) that comes up for you.

weekly tranquility tools

- ○ PLAN WEEK'S MITS
- ○ SOAK IN THE TUB
- ○ DIGITAL DAY OFF
- ○ CLEAR CLUTTER
- ○ PEN A LOVE NOTE
- ○ ARTIST DATE
- ○ GREEN JUICE
- ○ BUY OR PICK FRESH FLOWERS

WEEK 2: HOME, MIND, DIGITAL

Let's consider ways to declutter our homes, minds, and digital world and choose a few actions that resonate with you to try.

HOME

- Visualize how you want your space to look and feel.
- Schedule an hour, day, or weekend to declutter and start with the space that needs the most attention.
- Pull everything out of closets, drawers, shelves, and cabinets one area at a time.
- When debating what to keep, ask yourself, "Does this spark joy?" à la Marie Kondo.
- Purchase only necessities for one day, week, or month and notice what, if anything, you miss.
- Use the one in, one out rule—when you bring something new into the home that isn't a consumable, you shed one thing.
- If you haven't used something in one year, consider letting it go.
- Downsize by shedding the non-essentials.

MIND

- Clear your mind by writing things down—worries, to-dos, goals, groceries, wishes, meal planning, etc.
- Get clear on what's essential to you.
- Prioritize and then single task—do one thing at a time.
- Create space: breathe, journal, wander, forest bathe, slow down.
- Limit what information you're consuming.
- To alleviate decision-making fatigue and overwhelm, set routines—what to eat for breakfast, what to wear, how to start and end your day, staples to buy at the grocery store.
- Meditate. How-to videos in Tranquil Treasures at kimberlywilson.com/treasures.

DIGITAL

- Unsubscribe from everything you never read.
- Create one centralized spot for ideas, projects, and travel such as Evernote.
- When jotting something into your phone's notes section, transfer it later into your digital or analog planner so that it's not forgotten.
- Organize your computer's desktop.
- Remove apps you're not using from your computer and phone.
- Take a digital detox (no online usage) morning, day, or even weekend.
- Cull your inbox and archive that email backlog.
- Ditch non-essential notifications.
- Stick only to social media that brings you joy.
- Organize your photos and videos, then delete the extras.
- Delete contents of your downloads folder.
- Sort your files and folders to make documents easy to find.

weekly tranquility tools

- ○ PLAN WEEK'S MITS
- ○ PEN A LOVE NOTE
- ○ SOAK IN THE TUB
- ○ ARTIST DATE
- ○ DIGITAL DAY OFF
- ○ GREEN JUICE
- ○ CLEAR CLUTTER
- ○ BUY OR PICK FRESH FLOWERS

WEEK 3: TIME, ENERGY, MONEY

Using a minimalist lens, let's look at our usage of time, energy, and money. These are precious resources and the practices below offer ideas on using them in a way that reflects how we want to live (not how we think we should live).

1. **TAKE A SABBATH.** Consider a digital day off or leave your phone in the other room for a few hours. Skip TV to read a book, meditate, bake a pie, take a walk, or volunteer. Note what's keeping you from your priorities and take a break from them—answering the phone, replying immediately to emails and texts, paying attention to push notifications.

2. **SAY NO.** Although the tendency may be to raise your hand and take on that extra project, consider saying "No, thank you. Not right now." It will feel foreign and then, with practice, it will become empowering!

3. **ORGANIZE.** Review your planner and note superfluous plans, commitments, or to-dos. Can any be completely removed or rearranged to fit better with your energy level? I do this often when I realize I've added too many output activities and not enough input time. Also, note how much time you spend on relationships, hobbies, exercise, internet, watching TV, and alone. Does this match your values? No judgment, just notice.

4. **CREATE MITS.** This stands for Most Important Tasks and these are the items that

need to be completed due to deadlines, events, or priorities. Set 3–5 each day or each week (larger projects). This helps because then that long to-do list may not feel quite so overwhelming since your focus is on these few items.

5. **TRY THE POMODORO TECHNIQUE.** This time management system encourages people to work with the time they have by breaking the workday into 25-minute chunks separated by five-minute breaks. These intervals are referred to as pomodoros. After about four pomodoros, take a longer break of 15 to 20 minutes.

6. **BATCH TASKS/SINGLE TASK.** Batching means collecting a group of similar activities and doing them all at the same time. Batch replying to emails, household chores, reading assignments, or making videos, and do them at one time. When doing a task, avoid hopping from thing to thing. Let it be your sole focus. This helps maximize concentration and eliminate distraction.

7. **MINDFUL FOOD/DRINK.** Buy local. Tote your own tea/coffee to work. Invite friends over for dinner versus going out to eat. Try economical, healthy recipes (ideas on p. 37). Buy essentials in bulk. Meet friends for dessert versus an entire meal out. Grow your own food. Create a food budget.

8. **GO DIY.** Make your own cleaning products by blending two tablespoons white vinegar, ½ cup baking soda, ½ cup liquid Castile soap, 10 drops of lemon and peppermint essential oils, and ½ cup water. Create gifts for special occasions such as candles, granola, bath scrubs, peppermint spray, and baked goods.

9. **SHOPPING.** Skip browsing to invest in a few signature, quality pieces. Use what you have. Join the The Freecycle Network. Buy only essentials and consumables. Invest in experiences such as concerts, museum exhibits, and peony picking versus more stuff that has to be dusted. Before buying, ask yourself if it will bring you value now and in the future and if you really need it.

10. **SAVE.** Set aside as much as you can each month for your rainy day or retirement fund. Consider having 5–10 percent taken out of your paycheck before it hits your bank account so you won't be tempted to spend it all. Automate your payments to avoid late fees.

These are a few ways to incorporate the minimalist mindset into our time, energy, and spending habits while expanding our productivity, creativity, and savings account. Pick a few to try as you focus on what is most essential.

weekly tranquility tools

- PLAN WEEK'S MITS
- PEN A LOVE NOTE
- SOAK IN THE TUB
- ARTIST DATE
- DIGITAL DAY OFF
- GREEN JUICE
- CLEAR CLUTTER
- BUY OR PICK FRESH FLOWERS

4

WEEK 4: SIMPLIFY

Although we may not run off to the woods Thoreau style, we can hit the pause button from time to time to check in with ourselves. To live a more minimalist lifestyle—whatever that means to you—it's important that we take small steps to simplify our everyday lives.

This whole concept boils down to identifying what's important to you and eliminating the rest.

1. **LIMIT MEDIA CONSUMPTION.** According to the *New York Times*, Americans spend five hours watching TV and *Entrepreneur* notes that another two hours is spent on social media daily.

2. **ESTABLISH ROUTINES.** Housework, grocery shopping, bill payment, meals, morning and evening rituals, bathing, and travel prep.

3. **CREATE SPACE.** On your desk, in your life, in your schedule, in your handbag, and in your mind. Shed what's draining you—relationships, commitments, stuff.

4. **REFLECT.** Make a list of what you value most right now. Make sure they're getting time and space in your planner and in your day-to-day.

5. **CONTRIBUTE.** Volunteer, donate, raise awareness, support your favorite causes, host awareness-raising events, and be of service.

This month has been filled with tools, tips, and ideas on living a lifestyle that aligns most with what you hold dear. My hope is that you've found a couple of ideas to help bring more simplicity and ease to your every day.

Remember, there's no right or wrong way to practice minimalism. It's your interpretation of the minimalist movement that matters most. Identify what is important and begin to shed those non-essentials.

weekly tranquility tools

- ○ PLAN WEEK'S MITS
- ○ SOAK IN THE TUB
- ○ DIGITAL DAY OFF
- ○ CLEAR CLUTTER
- ○ PEN A LOVE NOTE
- ○ ARTIST DATE
- ○ GREEN JUICE
- ○ BUY OR PICK FRESH FLOWERS

monthly planner

MONTH: _____ **INTENTION:** _____

SUNDAY	MONDAY	TUESDAY	WEDNESDAY	THURSDAY	FRIDAY	SATURDAY

monthly tranquility tools and practices

- ○ CRAFT MONTH'S DREAMS
- ○ REVIEW BUDGET
- ○ WEEK 1

- ○ CREATE SOMETHING
- ○ READ TWO BOOKS
- ○ WEEK 2

- ○ VOLUNTEER
- ○ MANI/PEDI
- ○ WEEK 3

- ○ ENTERTAIN
- ○ MASSAGE
- ○ WEEK 4

month's dreams

month's review

moon phases

Notice your connection to the moon's cycles in these four phases: new, waxing, full, waning. Consider the prompts below as a way to tie into your Month's Dreams and provide space for monthly reflection.

new moon

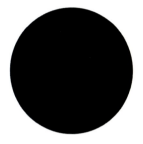

A TIME FOR SETTING INTENTIONS.
I WANT . . .

waxing moon

A TIME FOR ACTION.
I WILL . . .

full moon

A TIME FOR HARVEST AND CLOSURE.
I RELEASE . . .

waning moon

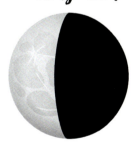

A TIME FOR SOFTENING.
I FEEL . . .

daily checklist

TRACK YOUR INCORPORATION OF THE DAILY TRANQUILITY TOOLS.

1
- MORNING ROUTINE
- DAILY DRESS-UP
- MINDFUL MOVEMENT
- EAT YOUR VEGGIES
- JOURNAL
- GOAL REVIEW
- GRATITUDE
- EVENING ROUTINE
- _____

2
- MORNING ROUTINE
- DAILY DRESS-UP
- MINDFUL MOVEMENT
- EAT YOUR VEGGIES
- JOURNAL
- GOAL REVIEW
- GRATITUDE
- EVENING ROUTINE
- _____

3
- MORNING ROUTINE
- DAILY DRESS-UP
- MINDFUL MOVEMENT
- EAT YOUR VEGGIES
- JOURNAL
- GOAL REVIEW
- GRATITUDE
- EVENING ROUTINE
- _____

4
- MORNING ROUTINE
- DAILY DRESS-UP
- MINDFUL MOVEMENT
- EAT YOUR VEGGIES
- JOURNAL
- GOAL REVIEW
- GRATITUDE
- EVENING ROUTINE
- _____

5
- MORNING ROUTINE
- DAILY DRESS-UP
- MINDFUL MOVEMENT
- EAT YOUR VEGGIES
- JOURNAL
- GOAL REVIEW
- GRATITUDE
- EVENING ROUTINE
- _____

6
- MORNING ROUTINE
- DAILY DRESS-UP
- MINDFUL MOVEMENT
- EAT YOUR VEGGIES
- JOURNAL
- GOAL REVIEW
- GRATITUDE
- EVENING ROUTINE
- _____

7
- MORNING ROUTINE
- DAILY DRESS-UP
- MINDFUL MOVEMENT
- EAT YOUR VEGGIES
- JOURNAL
- GOAL REVIEW
- GRATITUDE
- EVENING ROUTINE
- _____

8
- MORNING ROUTINE
- DAILY DRESS-UP
- MINDFUL MOVEMENT
- EAT YOUR VEGGIES
- JOURNAL
- GOAL REVIEW
- GRATITUDE
- EVENING ROUTINE
- _____

9
- MORNING ROUTINE
- DAILY DRESS-UP
- MINDFUL MOVEMENT
- EAT YOUR VEGGIES
- JOURNAL
- GOAL REVIEW
- GRATITUDE
- EVENING ROUTINE
- _____

10
- MORNING ROUTINE
- DAILY DRESS-UP
- MINDFUL MOVEMENT
- EAT YOUR VEGGIES
- JOURNAL
- GOAL REVIEW
- GRATITUDE
- EVENING ROUTINE
- _____

11
- MORNING ROUTINE
- DAILY DRESS-UP
- MINDFUL MOVEMENT
- EAT YOUR VEGGIES
- JOURNAL
- GOAL REVIEW
- GRATITUDE
- EVENING ROUTINE
- _____

12
- MORNING ROUTINE
- DAILY DRESS-UP
- MINDFUL MOVEMENT
- EAT YOUR VEGGIES
- JOURNAL
- GOAL REVIEW
- GRATITUDE
- EVENING ROUTINE
- _____

13
- MORNING ROUTINE
- DAILY DRESS-UP
- MINDFUL MOVEMENT
- EAT YOUR VEGGIES
- JOURNAL
- GOAL REVIEW
- GRATITUDE
- EVENING ROUTINE
- _____

14
- MORNING ROUTINE
- DAILY DRESS-UP
- MINDFUL MOVEMENT
- EAT YOUR VEGGIES
- JOURNAL
- GOAL REVIEW
- GRATITUDE
- EVENING ROUTINE
- _____

15
- MORNING ROUTINE
- DAILY DRESS-UP
- MINDFUL MOVEMENT
- EAT YOUR VEGGIES
- JOURNAL
- GOAL REVIEW
- GRATITUDE
- EVENING ROUTINE
- _____

16
- MORNING ROUTINE
- DAILY DRESS-UP
- MINDFUL MOVEMENT
- EAT YOUR VEGGIES
- JOURNAL
- GOAL REVIEW
- GRATITUDE
- EVENING ROUTINE
- _____

17
- MORNING ROUTINE
- DAILY DRESS-UP
- MINDFUL MOVEMENT
- EAT YOUR VEGGIES
- JOURNAL
- GOAL REVIEW
- GRATITUDE
- EVENING ROUTINE
- _____

18
- MORNING ROUTINE
- DAILY DRESS-UP
- MINDFUL MOVEMENT
- EAT YOUR VEGGIES
- JOURNAL
- GOAL REVIEW
- GRATITUDE
- EVENING ROUTINE
- _____

19
- MORNING ROUTINE
- DAILY DRESS-UP
- MINDFUL MOVEMENT
- EAT YOUR VEGGIES
- JOURNAL
- GOAL REVIEW
- GRATITUDE
- EVENING ROUTINE
- _____

20
- MORNING ROUTINE
- DAILY DRESS-UP
- MINDFUL MOVEMENT
- EAT YOUR VEGGIES
- JOURNAL
- GOAL REVIEW
- GRATITUDE
- EVENING ROUTINE
- _____

21
- MORNING ROUTINE
- DAILY DRESS-UP
- MINDFUL MOVEMENT
- EAT YOUR VEGGIES
- JOURNAL
- GOAL REVIEW
- GRATITUDE
- EVENING ROUTINE
- _____

22
- MORNING ROUTINE
- DAILY DRESS-UP
- MINDFUL MOVEMENT
- EAT YOUR VEGGIES
- JOURNAL
- GOAL REVIEW
- GRATITUDE
- EVENING ROUTINE
- _____

23
- MORNING ROUTINE
- DAILY DRESS-UP
- MINDFUL MOVEMENT
- EAT YOUR VEGGIES
- JOURNAL
- GOAL REVIEW
- GRATITUDE
- EVENING ROUTINE
- _____

24
- MORNING ROUTINE
- DAILY DRESS-UP
- MINDFUL MOVEMENT
- EAT YOUR VEGGIES
- JOURNAL
- GOAL REVIEW
- GRATITUDE
- EVENING ROUTINE
- _____

25
- MORNING ROUTINE
- DAILY DRESS-UP
- MINDFUL MOVEMENT
- EAT YOUR VEGGIES
- JOURNAL
- GOAL REVIEW
- GRATITUDE
- EVENING ROUTINE
- _____

26
- MORNING ROUTINE
- DAILY DRESS-UP
- MINDFUL MOVEMENT
- EAT YOUR VEGGIES
- JOURNAL
- GOAL REVIEW
- GRATITUDE
- EVENING ROUTINE
- _____

27
- MORNING ROUTINE
- DAILY DRESS-UP
- MINDFUL MOVEMENT
- EAT YOUR VEGGIES
- JOURNAL
- GOAL REVIEW
- GRATITUDE
- EVENING ROUTINE
- _____

28
- MORNING ROUTINE
- DAILY DRESS-UP
- MINDFUL MOVEMENT
- EAT YOUR VEGGIES
- JOURNAL
- GOAL REVIEW
- GRATITUDE
- EVENING ROUTINE
- _____

29
- MORNING ROUTINE
- DAILY DRESS-UP
- MINDFUL MOVEMENT
- EAT YOUR VEGGIES
- JOURNAL
- GOAL REVIEW
- GRATITUDE
- EVENING ROUTINE
- _____

30
- MORNING ROUTINE
- DAILY DRESS-UP
- MINDFUL MOVEMENT
- EAT YOUR VEGGIES
- JOURNAL
- GOAL REVIEW
- GRATITUDE
- EVENING ROUTINE
- _____

wellness

"THE CONCEPT OF TOTAL WELLNESS RECOGNIZES THAT OUR EVERY THOUGHT, WORD, AND BEHAVIOR AFFECTS OUR GREATER HEALTH AND WELL-BEING."
—GREG ANDERSON

The World Health Organization defines wellness as "a state of complete physical, mental, and social well-being, and not merely the absence of disease or infirmity."

When I sat down to pen this essay, I couldn't get the idea of our seasonal Life Review (p. 86) out of my head. Although we look at it during our seasonal *Tranquility du Jour Live* events, I thought it might be useful to review it along with this essay.

It's helpful to take a step back and review the big picture, versus focusing only on our day-to-day. This allows us to stay cognizant of what's working and what needs more attention. That's how I see wellness—a review of many areas of our life that contribute to the mind, body, and spiritual connection. The funny thing about wellness is that there isn't one way to practice it, it's an individual experience.

There are a few practices that I've incorporated into my lifestyle that have had a profound impact on my wellness such as having annual blood work, getting my teeth cleaned every six months, starting the day with hot water and lemon, practicing meditation, and moving my body regularly through walking, yoga, ballet, or biking.

And there are many areas where I can grow (a kind understatement) such as flossing my teeth daily, setting clear budgets, not getting worked up by the little things like traffic and slow walkers, and consuming too much sugar, to name a few.

According to the Institute for Wellness Education, there are 10 different areas of wellness and we'll cover each this month. Before researching this topic, I thought wellness was mainly eating good food, living a healthy lifestyle, and having good coping strategies.

Turns out it's that and so much more! Wellness for me has been a circuitous, meandering journey, and it continues to unfold as I learn more and become more self-aware. I'm sure you, too, can relate.

For years I subsisted on mainly sugary cereal and soymilk, was impulsive and reacted quickly to everyday triggers (have I mentioned traffic?), and gave into mindless shopping jaunts. None of these were good for my physical, emotional, or financial health.

Wellness is more about making conscious choices rather than operating on autopilot or impulse. We don't have to deprive ourselves of all treats, but we can become more mindful of what we choose and why. Use the Wellness Planning sheet on p. 34 to track habits and plan your meals and food shopping.

Practicing wellness is our chance to choose a response that reflects what's best for us. Sometimes it may be that new vegan cookie at Starbucks, other times it may be freshly baked kale chips.

As you move through this month focusing on wellness, take note of your everyday decisions. From what you put into your body, how you move (or don't move), what you focus on, how you feel, what triggers you, your social support system, your core values, your spending habits, your physical surroundings, and your work performance and ask yourself, "Does this contribute to wellness?"

Try out a few new tools, consider some habits you may want to shift, and keep those bigger intentions in mind. Get ready for a month filled with support and encouragement to live a life peppered with goodness. Author Deborah Day wrote, "Nourishing yourself in a way that helps you blossom in the direction you want to go is attainable, and you are worth the effort." These wellness practices will help get you there!

Savvy Sources

BOOKS:
Eat Pretty by Jolene Hart
The Gifts of Imperfection by Brene Brown
Thrive by Arianna Huffington
The Wellness Project by Phoebe Lapine
Main Street Vegan by Victoria Moran
The Feeling Good Handbook by David D. Burns, M.D.
The Nature Fix by Florence Williams

APPS:
Sleep Cycle
My Possible Self

TRANQUILITY DU JOUR PODCASTS:
#181 Living The Not So Big Life
#240 Main Street Vegan
#335 Walk On the Healthy Side
#370 Tea Wellness
#397 Nourish 360
#398 Make Peace with Your Mind
#421 From Anxiety to Love

notes:

1

WEEK 1: PHYSICAL, NUTRITIONAL, MEDICAL

PHYSICAL

Consider your daily physical activity and notice any areas for improvement. Park further away from the entrance, take the stairs, walk your dog on a longer route, or bike to work.

Maintain a regular sleep schedule and shoot for 7–9 hours each night. If you're struggling with sleep, see someone to discuss the issue. It's hard to be our best when we're missing the basics.

Track your steps via a Fitbit or your phone and reward yourself when making the recommended 10k/day.

Try a new form of movement such as yoga (next month's focus), dance, tennis, jumping rope, biking, running, barre, hiking, or jogging and strive for 30 minutes of daily physical activity. Check out studios' intro specials to dip your toe in.

NUTRITIONAL

Keep a log of what you eat and notice how you feel when eating processed or packaged products versus whole foods.

Add more colorful, nutrient-dense foods to your plate such as dark leafy greens, cauliflower, sweet potatoes, nuts, seeds, blueberries, black beans, and tomatoes.

Stock your kitchen with plant-based foods and try a detox (p. 36).

Pack a nutritious lunch or midday snacks to avoid vending machines or takeout temptation.

Try to keep your added sugar intake around 25 grams per day. Note the sugar content in energy drinks, lattes, juices, and sodas.

MEDICAL/DENTAL

- Schedule your annual physical.
- Consider alternative therapies such as massage, acupuncture, or an herbalist.
- Stay up-to-date with your prescriptions and set up automatic refills to avoid running out.
- Visit the dentist every six months.
- Talk with a therapist.
- If anything is feeling out of sorts, make an appointment to get it checked out.

Review these suggestions and add one from each category to your week.

weekly tranquility tools

- ○ PLAN WEEK'S MITS
- ○ PEN A LOVE NOTE
- ○ SOAK IN THE TUB
- ○ ARTIST DATE
- ○ DIGITAL DAY OFF
- ○ GREEN JUICE
- ○ CLEAR CLUTTER
- ○ BUY OR PICK FRESH FLOWERS

WEEK 2: SPIRITUAL, SOCIAL, ENVIRONMENTAL

SPIRITUAL

- Volunteer and contribute through community service.
- Do more of what offers you a sense of meaning and purpose (see Meaning).
- Pray, meditate, or be still.
- Spend time in nature.
- Attend events that delight such as the performing arts.
- Read texts and listen to music and podcasts that inspire you.
- Practice gratitude.

SOCIAL

- Build and sustain healthy relationships (see Love).
- Invite someone to brunch or tea.
- Treat others with tender care and remember the Golden Rule.
- To expand your connections and interests, join a like-hearted club or organization, or start your own.
- Practice clear and compassionate communication and set healthy boundaries.
- Remember loved ones' special days and send "thinking of you" notes to friends and family.
- Be fully present with the person in front of you.

ENVIRONMENTAL

- Eat locally and with the seasons.
- Forgo plastic and tote your own water bottle.
- Keep your surroundings clutter-free and pleasing to your senses.
- Plant and tend a community garden.
- Skip products with lots of packaging.
- Strive for zero waste: refuse what you don't need, reduce what you use, reuse what you have, repair when possible, recycle.
- Eliminate as much trash as possible from the household.
- Use glass jars over plastic containers.
- Tote cloth bags to the store.
- Try multi-purpose products such as Dr. Bronner's Pure-Castile Liquid Soap.
- Upcycle by repurposing old items into new ones such as a tee into a tote.

Review these suggestions and add one from each category to your week.

weekly tranquility tools

- ○ PLAN WEEK'S MITS
- ○ SOAK IN THE TUB
- ○ DIGITAL DAY OFF
- ○ CLEAR CLUTTER
- ○ PEN A LOVE NOTE
- ○ ARTIST DATE
- ○ GREEN JUICE
- ○ BUY OR PICK FRESH FLOWERS

GREEN SMOOTHIES, MANI PEDI, BUBBLE BATHS, AND **CHANGE THE WORLD.**

WEEK 3: EMOTIONAL AND OCCUPATIONAL

EMOTIONAL

An emotion is thoughts plus bodily sensations. Try to name the emotion and feel it in your body. Give voice to your emotions.

Polish those coping skills. Meditate, journal, reframe problems to find solutions, repeat "cancel, cancel" to those negative thoughts on replay and replace them with a positive thought, recognize cognitive distortions like overgeneralizing (assuming all future experiences will be the same based on an isolated incident) or catastrophizing (seeing the worst in situations).

Keep the bigger picture in mind.

Practice relaxation and soothing techniques such as legs up the wall, soaking in the tub, or listening to classical music.

Practice positivity and gratitude.

Pay attention to triggers.

When triggered, practice STOP: Stop, Take a breath, Observe what's happening, Proceed with awareness. This helps to respond versus react.

Indulge in activities that nurture your senses such as using an aromatherapy diffuser, playing with your pet or child, wrapping yourself in a chunky knit blanket, listening to music, and savoring a cup of tea or pot of vegan chili.

OCCUPATIONAL

- Work with your strengths and deepen your communication skills.
- Consider your interests and build new skills.
- Build connections with colleagues.
- Design an inspiring workspace: plants, standing desk, bags of tea, lavender oil, snacks, images/colors/fabrics that inspire.
- Seek personal satisfaction and enrichment in life through meaningful work inside or outside of the home (see Meaning).
- Straddle that sweet spot between work and play.
- Strive to keep moving forward by using primers and accountability partners (see Dreams).

Review these suggestions and add one from each category to your week.

weekly tranquility tools

- ○ PLAN WEEK'S MITS
- ○ PEN A LOVE NOTE
- ○ SOAK IN THE TUB
- ○ ARTIST DATE
- ○ DIGITAL DAY OFF
- ○ GREEN JUICE
- ○ CLEAR CLUTTER
- ○ BUY OR PICK FRESH FLOWERS

WEEK 4: FINANCIAL AND BEHAVIORAL

BEHAVIORAL

- Expand your horizons—road trip, documentary, museum, art gallery, live music, theater.
- Be a lifelong learner. Take classes, attend workshops, watch videos, and read all you can.
- Shake it up by doing things differently.
- Track your habits and notice what small shifts may contribute to a healthier lifestyle.
- Attend a lecture, book signing, or workshop to learn and grow.
- Try an assortment of DIY projects such as candle or jewelry making or consider a new hobby such as ballroom dancing or photography.
- Seek out challenges—try a puzzle app, cut out caffeine or alcohol, learn a new language, try Tai Chi, learn to play the ukulele, read and memorize poetry, take a pottery class.

FINANCIAL

- Note your weekly spending habits (p. 41).
- Create a monthly household budget and review it regularly (p. 40).
- Consult with a financial advisor to set up your retirement plan.
- Set up a savings account and have money automatically put into it each month. Build an emergency fund.
- Pack your lunch and a few snacks instead of going out to eat. You'll eat healthier and save money.
- Skip unnecessary expenses by buying only essentials and/or consumables for a day, week, month, or more.
- Just say no to credit card debt and try to live within your means. No pair of shoes is worth 15 percent interest. Promise! Keep that credit score strong.
- Shop second hand, check out bartering and swapping websites, and visit the library for your bibliophilia needs.
- Consider a side hustle. This is a second job that brings in income and allows you the flexibility to work your regular job. (More in Entrepreneurship).
- Donate to charities that you love.

Review these suggestions and add one from each category to your week.

weekly tranquility tools

- ○ PLAN WEEK'S MITS
- ○ PEN A LOVE NOTE
- ○ SOAK IN THE TUB
- ○ ARTIST DATE
- ○ DIGITAL DAY OFF
- ○ GREEN JUICE
- ○ CLEAR CLUTTER
- ○ BUY OR PICK FRESH FLOWERS

seasonal life review

DATE: _____

SEASONALLY REFLECT ON AREAS OF YOUR LIFE. RATE EACH ONE WITH YOUR LEVEL OF SATISFACTION 10 = BLISS, 5 = SO-SO, 0 = BOO.

Here are some additional areas to consider: social life, romance, family, education, health, fitness, meaning, activism. Next, take a moment to note the areas that ranked low and create three action steps to increase your tranquility in these areas. Be gentle. Plant seeds. Watch dreams take root.

ACTION STEPS TO INCREASE AREAS THAT ARE LOWER THAN I'D LIKE:

seasonal checklist

- ○ WHEEL OF LIFE
- ○ BED DAY
- ○ DEEP CLEAN
- ○ REARRANGE
- ○ PRACTICE ESSENTIALISM
- ○ GET CULTURED
- ○ TRY SOMETHING NEW
- ○ TEND YOUR GARDEN
- ○ _____

monthly planner

MONTH: _____ INTENTION: _____

SUNDAY	MONDAY	TUESDAY	WEDNESDAY	THURSDAY	FRIDAY	SATURDAY

monthly tranquility tools and practices

- ○ CRAFT MONTH'S DREAMS
- ○ REVIEW BUDGET
- ○ WEEK 1
- ○ CREATE SOMETHING
- ○ READ TWO BOOKS
- ○ WEEK 2
- ○ VOLUNTEER
- ○ MANI/PEDI
- ○ WEEK 3
- ○ ENTERTAIN
- ○ MASSAGE
- ○ WEEK 4

month's dreams

month's review

moon phases

Notice your connection to the moon's cycles in these four phases: *new, waxing, full, waning*. Consider the prompts below as a way to tie into your Month's Dreams and provide space for monthly reflection.

new moon

waxing moon

A TIME FOR SETTING INTENTIONS.
I WANT...

A TIME FOR ACTION.
I WILL...

full moon

waning moon

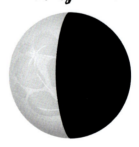

A TIME FOR HARVEST AND CLOSURE.
I RELEASE...

A TIME FOR SOFTENING.
I FEEL...

daily checklist

TRACK YOUR INCORPORATION OF THE DAILY TRANQUILITY TOOLS.

Day 1
- ○ MORNING ROUTINE
- ○ DAILY DRESS-UP
- ○ MINDFUL MOVEMENT
- ○ EAT YOUR VEGGIES
- ○ JOURNAL
- ○ GOAL REVIEW
- ○ GRATITUDE
- ○ EVENING ROUTINE
- ○ _____

Day 2
- ○ MORNING ROUTINE
- ○ DAILY DRESS-UP
- ○ MINDFUL MOVEMENT
- ○ EAT YOUR VEGGIES
- ○ JOURNAL
- ○ GOAL REVIEW
- ○ GRATITUDE
- ○ EVENING ROUTINE
- ○ _____

Day 3
- ○ MORNING ROUTINE
- ○ DAILY DRESS-UP
- ○ MINDFUL MOVEMENT
- ○ EAT YOUR VEGGIES
- ○ JOURNAL
- ○ GOAL REVIEW
- ○ GRATITUDE
- ○ EVENING ROUTINE
- ○ _____

Day 4
- ○ MORNING ROUTINE
- ○ DAILY DRESS-UP
- ○ MINDFUL MOVEMENT
- ○ EAT YOUR VEGGIES
- ○ JOURNAL
- ○ GOAL REVIEW
- ○ GRATITUDE
- ○ EVENING ROUTINE
- ○ _____

Day 5
- ○ MORNING ROUTINE
- ○ DAILY DRESS-UP
- ○ MINDFUL MOVEMENT
- ○ EAT YOUR VEGGIES
- ○ JOURNAL
- ○ GOAL REVIEW
- ○ GRATITUDE
- ○ EVENING ROUTINE
- ○ _____

Day 6
- ○ MORNING ROUTINE
- ○ DAILY DRESS-UP
- ○ MINDFUL MOVEMENT
- ○ EAT YOUR VEGGIES
- ○ JOURNAL
- ○ GOAL REVIEW
- ○ GRATITUDE
- ○ EVENING ROUTINE
- ○ _____

Day 7
- ○ MORNING ROUTINE
- ○ DAILY DRESS-UP
- ○ MINDFUL MOVEMENT
- ○ EAT YOUR VEGGIES
- ○ JOURNAL
- ○ GOAL REVIEW
- ○ GRATITUDE
- ○ EVENING ROUTINE
- ○ _____

Day 8
- ○ MORNING ROUTINE
- ○ DAILY DRESS-UP
- ○ MINDFUL MOVEMENT
- ○ EAT YOUR VEGGIES
- ○ JOURNAL
- ○ GOAL REVIEW
- ○ GRATITUDE
- ○ EVENING ROUTINE
- ○ _____

Day 9
- ○ MORNING ROUTINE
- ○ DAILY DRESS-UP
- ○ MINDFUL MOVEMENT
- ○ EAT YOUR VEGGIES
- ○ JOURNAL
- ○ GOAL REVIEW
- ○ GRATITUDE
- ○ EVENING ROUTINE
- ○ _____

Day 10
- ○ MORNING ROUTINE
- ○ DAILY DRESS-UP
- ○ MINDFUL MOVEMENT
- ○ EAT YOUR VEGGIES
- ○ JOURNAL
- ○ GOAL REVIEW
- ○ GRATITUDE
- ○ EVENING ROUTINE
- ○ _____

Day 11
- ○ MORNING ROUTINE
- ○ DAILY DRESS-UP
- ○ MINDFUL MOVEMENT
- ○ EAT YOUR VEGGIES
- ○ JOURNAL
- ○ GOAL REVIEW
- ○ GRATITUDE
- ○ EVENING ROUTINE
- ○ _____

Day 12
- ○ MORNING ROUTINE
- ○ DAILY DRESS-UP
- ○ MINDFUL MOVEMENT
- ○ EAT YOUR VEGGIES
- ○ JOURNAL
- ○ GOAL REVIEW
- ○ GRATITUDE
- ○ EVENING ROUTINE
- ○ _____

Day 13
- ○ MORNING ROUTINE
- ○ DAILY DRESS-UP
- ○ MINDFUL MOVEMENT
- ○ EAT YOUR VEGGIES
- ○ JOURNAL
- ○ GOAL REVIEW
- ○ GRATITUDE
- ○ EVENING ROUTINE
- ○ _____

Day 14
- ○ MORNING ROUTINE
- ○ DAILY DRESS-UP
- ○ MINDFUL MOVEMENT
- ○ EAT YOUR VEGGIES
- ○ JOURNAL
- ○ GOAL REVIEW
- ○ GRATITUDE
- ○ EVENING ROUTINE
- ○ _____

Day 15
- ○ MORNING ROUTINE
- ○ DAILY DRESS-UP
- ○ MINDFUL MOVEMENT
- ○ EAT YOUR VEGGIES
- ○ JOURNAL
- ○ GOAL REVIEW
- ○ GRATITUDE
- ○ EVENING ROUTINE
- ○ _____

Day 16
- ○ MORNING ROUTINE
- ○ DAILY DRESS-UP
- ○ MINDFUL MOVEMENT
- ○ EAT YOUR VEGGIES
- ○ JOURNAL
- ○ GOAL REVIEW
- ○ GRATITUDE
- ○ EVENING ROUTINE
- ○ _____

Day 17
- ○ MORNING ROUTINE
- ○ DAILY DRESS-UP
- ○ MINDFUL MOVEMENT
- ○ EAT YOUR VEGGIES
- ○ JOURNAL
- ○ GOAL REVIEW
- ○ GRATITUDE
- ○ EVENING ROUTINE
- ○ _____

Day 18
- ○ MORNING ROUTINE
- ○ DAILY DRESS-UP
- ○ MINDFUL MOVEMENT
- ○ EAT YOUR VEGGIES
- ○ JOURNAL
- ○ GOAL REVIEW
- ○ GRATITUDE
- ○ EVENING ROUTINE
- ○ _____

Day 19
- ○ MORNING ROUTINE
- ○ DAILY DRESS-UP
- ○ MINDFUL MOVEMENT
- ○ EAT YOUR VEGGIES
- ○ JOURNAL
- ○ GOAL REVIEW
- ○ GRATITUDE
- ○ EVENING ROUTINE
- ○ _____

Day 20
- ○ MORNING ROUTINE
- ○ DAILY DRESS-UP
- ○ MINDFUL MOVEMENT
- ○ EAT YOUR VEGGIES
- ○ JOURNAL
- ○ GOAL REVIEW
- ○ GRATITUDE
- ○ EVENING ROUTINE
- ○ _____

Day 21
- ○ MORNING ROUTINE
- ○ DAILY DRESS-UP
- ○ MINDFUL MOVEMENT
- ○ EAT YOUR VEGGIES
- ○ JOURNAL
- ○ GOAL REVIEW
- ○ GRATITUDE
- ○ EVENING ROUTINE
- ○ _____

Day 22
- ○ MORNING ROUTINE
- ○ DAILY DRESS-UP
- ○ MINDFUL MOVEMENT
- ○ EAT YOUR VEGGIES
- ○ JOURNAL
- ○ GOAL REVIEW
- ○ GRATITUDE
- ○ EVENING ROUTINE
- ○ _____

Day 23
- ○ MORNING ROUTINE
- ○ DAILY DRESS-UP
- ○ MINDFUL MOVEMENT
- ○ EAT YOUR VEGGIES
- ○ JOURNAL
- ○ GOAL REVIEW
- ○ GRATITUDE
- ○ EVENING ROUTINE
- ○ _____

Day 24
- ○ MORNING ROUTINE
- ○ DAILY DRESS-UP
- ○ MINDFUL MOVEMENT
- ○ EAT YOUR VEGGIES
- ○ JOURNAL
- ○ GOAL REVIEW
- ○ GRATITUDE
- ○ EVENING ROUTINE
- ○ _____

Day 25
- ○ MORNING ROUTINE
- ○ DAILY DRESS-UP
- ○ MINDFUL MOVEMENT
- ○ EAT YOUR VEGGIES
- ○ JOURNAL
- ○ GOAL REVIEW
- ○ GRATITUDE
- ○ EVENING ROUTINE
- ○ _____

Day 26
- ○ MORNING ROUTINE
- ○ DAILY DRESS-UP
- ○ MINDFUL MOVEMENT
- ○ EAT YOUR VEGGIES
- ○ JOURNAL
- ○ GOAL REVIEW
- ○ GRATITUDE
- ○ EVENING ROUTINE
- ○ _____

Day 27
- ○ MORNING ROUTINE
- ○ DAILY DRESS-UP
- ○ MINDFUL MOVEMENT
- ○ EAT YOUR VEGGIES
- ○ JOURNAL
- ○ GOAL REVIEW
- ○ GRATITUDE
- ○ EVENING ROUTINE
- ○ _____

Day 28
- ○ MORNING ROUTINE
- ○ DAILY DRESS-UP
- ○ MINDFUL MOVEMENT
- ○ EAT YOUR VEGGIES
- ○ JOURNAL
- ○ GOAL REVIEW
- ○ GRATITUDE
- ○ EVENING ROUTINE
- ○ _____

Day 29
- ○ MORNING ROUTINE
- ○ DAILY DRESS-UP
- ○ MINDFUL MOVEMENT
- ○ EAT YOUR VEGGIES
- ○ JOURNAL
- ○ GOAL REVIEW
- ○ GRATITUDE
- ○ EVENING ROUTINE
- ○ _____

Day 30
- ○ MORNING ROUTINE
- ○ DAILY DRESS-UP
- ○ MINDFUL MOVEMENT
- ○ EAT YOUR VEGGIES
- ○ JOURNAL
- ○ GOAL REVIEW
- ○ GRATITUDE
- ○ EVENING ROUTINE
- ○ _____

Yoga

"YOGA DOES NOT REMOVE US FROM THE REALITY OR RESPONSIBILITIES OF EVERYDAY LIFE BUT RATHER PLACES OUR FEET FIRMLY AND RESOLUTELY IN THE PRACTICAL GROUND OF EXPERIENCE. WE DON'T TRANSCEND OUR LIVES; WE RETURN TO THE LIFE WE LEFT BEHIND IN THE HOPES OF SOMETHING BETTER." —DONNA FARHI

With views of Colorado's snow-capped mountains, freshly fallen snow glistened and the sun started to peek out as I drove toward Colorado's Silverthorne Recreation Center in 1996 with a childhood friend.

We were there to try yoga. The multipurpose room was a cold shell painted in grey with a beige rubber floor. We scattered our thick blue foam exercise mats across the rubbery surface to face floor-to-ceiling windows with the Rockies as our backdrop. A few retirees strolled in to join the class.

The teacher arrived—middle-aged, wearing colorful baggy clothing with a ponytail sitting atop her head. Tentative, I settled into a cross-legged seated position and decided to make the most of the experience. She told us to close our eyes and breathe.

I drifted back to her voice encouraging us to settle in. "Inhallleeeee, exhalllllle," she repeated over and over again. "Find your center. Let go of distractions. Notice your breath." I opened my eyes to peek. She appeared serene, still, and confident. I wanted some of that.

We transitioned to our hands and knees for spinal stretches in cat and cow poses—back and forth rounding and arching of the spine and breathing through the nose. We started by holding the poses for 10 seconds and then sped up to quick cat and cow movements with a "skull shining" breath of explosive exhales and passive inhales. The teacher gushed about clearing emotional debris and blockages between higher and lower chakras. Huh?

Next, we moved to downward-facing dog. I'd seen this pose peppered throughout women's magazines touting yoga as the *en vogue* exercise to tone the body and calm the mind. Moving into sun salutations, I liked the hip-opening lunges and the beads of perspiration that formed on my forehead from this dance-like sequence.

My mind quieted and my body opened. I found a chance to connect, feel, and nurture my body. I'd spent years trying not to feel, and this practice was all about feeling—physical sensations and emotions. There was a sense of coming home.

In the closing backbends I felt pulsing in my heart center similar to that fluttery feeling when meeting a lover. When we came to rest on our backs for the final pose, savasana, I exhaled and felt at ease for the first time in years.

Soon we wiggled our fingers and toes, and then rolled up to a cross-legged seated pose for the finale. I bowed my head, placed my hands to prayer position and the teacher said, "Namaste."

On a chilly evening in October 1999—a night I'd been anticipating since posting the ad under "Instruction" in the *Washington City Paper*—I anxiously readied my space. Interested strangers were en route to the first yoga class in my living room.

To prepare my small apartment, a fourth-floor walkup, I had vacuumed cat hair off the carpet before setting five emerald green sticky mats into a semi-circle in front of the fireplace. I printed inspiring quotes by Rumi, Buddha, and *Simple Abundance*'s Sarah Ban Breathnach onto pastel paper. On the center of each mat, I placed the sheet of quotes and a new student form rolled into scrolls secured with organza ribbons. I turned '90s fitness guru Denise Austin's instrumental cassette tape on repeat, lit a fire, and displayed scented candles on windowsills and bookshelves. This became my makeshift yoga studio.

At 6 p.m., I headed into the kitchen to brew chai tea from scratch. I set out the ingredients—cloves, black tea, cinnamon sticks, whole black peppercorns, sugar, and milk—and finished just in time to pour the chai into a thermos and set out a plate of cookies. Then I heard the buzzer.

The yogis arrived one by one. We started with meditation, gentle stretching and sun salutes, a few standing poses and tree, and made our way back to the floor. The session ended with a long relaxation topped with eye pillows, aromatherapy spray, and a rolled blanket under their knees.

After their relaxation, we gathered around the fireplace for chai and cookies. That evening Tranquil Space was born.

Yoga became my life for nearly two decades and I've found the benefits to be profound. Although I sold Tranquil Space to YogaWorks in 2017, I haven't let go of being a yoga evangelist. The benefits are extensive—relaxation, flexibility, muscle strength, focus, peace of mind. Yoga is a sacred way to connect to our bodies, our minds, and ourselves.

For example, there are eight limbs of yoga philosophy that help guide us ethically and numerous types of yoga and styles of teachers to align with varied personalities and preferences. Some find the practice to be life changing on many levels while others simply enjoy stretching their body into various poses.

There is no one correct way to practice yoga and what draws us to the mat varies from person to person. This month we'll explore why yoga can be so much more than stretching (if you're looking for more), ways to incorporate yoga into daily life, and how to become more aware of our body.

As Mariel Hemingway says, "Yoga teaches you how to listen to your body." Let's tune in, shall we?

Savvy Sources

BOOKS:
Hip Tranquil Chick by Kimberly Wilson
The Magic Ten and Beyond by Sharon Gannon
Jivamukti Yoga by Sharon Gannon and David Life
Living Your Yoga by Judith Lasater
Bringing Yoga to Life by Donna Farhi
The Yamas and Niyamas by Deborah Adele

APPS:
Yoga Studio
Yoga Poses

TRANQUILITY DU JOUR PODCASTS:
#126 Living Your Yoga
#194 A Life Worth Breathing
#246 Yoga Philosophy
#307 Yoga + Creativity
#315 Picking Your Practice
#355 Restorative Yoga Therapy
#425 The Magic Ten

notes:

1
WEEK 1: SUN SALUTATION

Let's try for a daily sun salutation. It will take approximately one minute. This practice works the entire body in a gentle, supportive way by stimulating the glands, nurturing the nervous system, loosening the muscles, and more!

You can try these in a group class, with a private teacher, while listening to an audio how-to, or watching a video at home. Choose what allows you to feel most comfortable—some days we may crave community while others may leave us longing for privacy. All you need is a yoga mat, stretchy clothing, and a desire to be in your body.

Here's how to move through a sun salutation:

1. Come to mountain pose at the top of the mat. Feel your feet grounded firmly. Set an intention.

2. Inhale, reach your arms to the sky.

3. Exhale, trace the midline of your body through prayer position and into a forward fold.

4. Inhale, step back with your right leg to a lunge.

5. Exhale, step back with your left leg to downward-facing dog (an inverted "V").

6. Inhale, float forward to plank pose. Align your shoulders over your wrists and wiggle your feet back so your heels are over the balls of your feet. If this is too much on your wrists, drop your knees.

7. Exhale, drop your knees, bend your arms to a 90-degree angle, hug your elbows into your body, and lower down so that your shoulders and hips are in a straight line for half-chaturanga.

8. Inhale, uncurl your toes, drop your belly, lift your heart center, and slide into cobra. Relax your shoulders from your ears.

9. Exhale, curl your toes under, and lift your hips up and back into downward-facing dog.

10. Inhale, step forward with your right foot.

11. Exhale, step your left foot between both hands to a forward fold.

12. Inhale, trace your midline to the sky.

13. Exhale, place your hands to prayer position in front of your heart. Repeat on the opposite side (step back with the left leg).

Try at least one daily sun salutation all month.

weekly tranquility tools

- ○ PLAN WEEK'S MITS
- ○ PEN A LOVE NOTE
- ○ SOAK IN THE TUB
- ○ ARTIST DATE
- ○ DIGITAL DAY OFF
- ○ GREEN JUICE
- ○ CLEAR CLUTTER
- ○ BUY OR PICK FRESH FLOWERS

WEEK 2: EIGHT YOGIC PRINCIPLES

1. YAMAS

The five yamas are considered the yogic don'ts or restraints and serve as the ethical foundation of the eight-fold path.

- **AHIMSA:** Non-violence. Make choices that don't cause violence through thoughts, words, and actions. Eat veg. Avoid gossip. Practice kindness.

- **SATYA:** Truthfulness. Be honest. Speak and live your authentic truth. Share who you really are—eccentricities and all.

- **ASTEYA:** Nonstealing. Avoid taking time, energy, and joy from yourself and others. Give credit. Be punctual and prepared.

- **BRAMACHARYA:** Moderation. Try the middle path. Appreciate what you have. Avoid excess. Learn what the body needs.

- **APARIGRAHA:** Nongrasping. Avoid taking more than you need through hoarding or accumulating and seek ways to give of yourself. Release control and surrender expectations.

2. NIYAMAS

The niyamas are the yogic dos or observances that include actions and attitudes to cultivate to reduce suffering.

- **SAUCHA:** Purity. Keep your mind and body clean inside and out by paying close attention to what you ingest. Maintain a tidy and orderly environment.

- **SAMTOSHA:** Contentment. Try to accept life and others as they are. Maintain a sense of gratitude.

- **TAPAS:** Discipline. Put ongoing effort into life, work, play, and in relationships. Make conscious choices that offer long-term benefits.

- **SVADYAYA:** Self-study. Get to know yourself through your practice, journaling, meditation, therapy, writing, reading, and relationships. Read sacred texts.

- **ISVARA PRANIDHANA:** Surrender to God. Let go and soften. Give of yourself to others. Release control.

3. ASANA: Physical poses to still the mind and awaken the body.

4. PRANAYAMA: Breathwork. Use the breath as a tool for connecting to the present moment.

5. PRATYAHARA: Withdrawal of the senses allows you to experience chaos without getting overwhelmed.

6. DHARANA: Concentration by being fully present.

7. DHYANA: Meditation.

8. SAMADHI: Bliss. This happens when you're in the flow, absorbed in the moment, and feel a connection to all living things.

Consider these eight parts of yoga. What interests you? Surprises you? Challenges you?

weekly tranquility tools

○ PLAN WEEK'S MITS
○ PEN A LOVE NOTE
○ SOAK IN THE TUB
○ ARTIST DATE
○ DIGITAL DAY OFF
○ GREEN JUICE
○ CLEAR CLUTTER
○ BUY OR PICK FRESH FLOWERS

WEEK 3: BREATHE

Without getting all fancy on you, I'm encouraging the exploration of a basic three-part breath (dirgha pranayama) throughout the week.

Our breath serves as a tool for coming into the present moment and eases stress, calms the nervous system, increases focus, and increases oxygen to the blood. And the best part, we always have it with us. No need to roll out a yoga mat or put on stretchy clothing.

Begin by finding a comfortable seat and breathe naturally for a few moments.

Next, draw the breath in through your nose and fill your belly, ribs, and chest with air. Then exhale and release your chest, ribs, and belly.

If you can't quite feel one of these parts (often the belly), place your hand there and try to move it with your breath. That's the best way to find those tricky parts.

Continue this breath for a few minutes.

No one has to know you're doing this. If you're dealing with a delayed flight, a tough conference call, a crying baby, or barking dog, this is a great go-to. Try this practice (the fourth limb of yoga) throughout the week a few times a day and watch your body and mind soften. Notice your breath this week.

weekly tranquility tools

- PLAN WEEK'S MITS
- PEN A LOVE NOTE
- SOAK IN THE TUB
- ARTIST DATE
- DIGITAL DAY OFF
- GREEN JUICE
- CLEAR CLUTTER
- BUY OR PICK FRESH FLOWERS

4 WEEK 4: OFF THE MAT

Let's consider the various yoga tools we've explored so far this month: sun salutations, how to utilize the yamas and niyamas, the eight limbs of yoga, and the three-part yogic breath. These are all tools and philosophies to support the practice.

This week I'd like to explore what yoga OFF the mat means.

In the early days of my yoga studio, Tranquil Space, I emphasized the importance of practicing yoga on AND off the yoga mat. If you consider the 10 yamas and niyamas, it can be helpful to ponder which of these would most benefit you right now. Yes, this moment.

Is it more discipline that's needed? Or is it being honest with yourself about a difficult situation? What about contentment and appreciating what you have?

Yoga off the mat goes beyond these 10 foundational tenets to infuse every part of our lives. When we're one person on the yoga mat—spiritual, grounded, kind—and another off the mat, we're out of alignment.

Practicing yoga beyond the mat includes how we treat other beings, the environment, and ourselves (more in Self-Care).

If you were to take the dedication of your spiritual practice (whether you're a regular yoga practitioner or not) into the world, how would that look? What would you do more of? Less of?

For example, I had *Lokah Samastah Sukhino Bhavantu* tattooed on my arm in 2011 and it serves as a reminder to be kind. Sharon Gannon, co-founder of Jivamukti yoga, translates the mantra as: May all beings everywhere be happy and free. May the thoughts, words, and actions of my own life contribute in some way to that happiness and to that freedom for all.

Not that you need a tattoo or that I no longer get rattled because of it, but having that reminder of what my yoga practice really means has served as a gentle nudge when I need it most.

Yoga off the mat is what matters. It's not about the perfect headstand or sweaty vinyasa class. It's about transforming through our spiritual practice in a way that benefits all.

This week consider how your spiritual practice shows up off the mat in daily life. How does it align with who you are and who you want to be?

weekly tranquility tools

- ○ PLAN WEEK'S MITS
- ○ PEN A LOVE NOTE
- ○ SOAK IN THE TUB
- ○ ARTIST DATE
- ○ DIGITAL DAY OFF
- ○ GREEN JUICE
- ○ CLEAR CLUTTER
- ○ BUY OR PICK FRESH FLOWERS

monthly planner

MONTH: _____   INTENTION: _____

SUNDAY	MONDAY	TUESDAY	WEDNESDAY	THURSDAY	FRIDAY	SATURDAY

monthly tranquility tools and practices

- ○ CRAFT MONTH'S DREAMS
- ○ REVIEW BUDGET
- ○ WEEK 1
- ○ CREATE SOMETHING
- ○ READ TWO BOOKS
- ○ WEEK 2
- ○ VOLUNTEER
- ○ MANI/PEDI
- ○ WEEK 3
- ○ ENTERTAIN
- ○ MASSAGE
- ○ WEEK 4

month's dreams

month's review

moon phases

Notice your connection to the moon's cycles in these four phases: new, waxing, full, waning. Consider the prompts below as a way to tie into your Month's Dreams and provide space for monthly reflection.

new moon

waxing moon

A TIME FOR SETTING INTENTIONS.
I WANT...

A TIME FOR ACTION.
I WILL...

full moon

waning moon

A TIME FOR HARVEST AND CLOSURE.
I RELEASE...

A TIME FOR SOFTENING.
I FEEL...

daily checklist

TRACK YOUR INCORPORATION OF THE DAILY TRANQUILITY TOOLS.

1
- MORNING ROUTINE
- DAILY DRESS-UP
- MINDFUL MOVEMENT
- EAT YOUR VEGGIES
- JOURNAL
- GOAL REVIEW
- GRATITUDE
- EVENING ROUTINE

2
- MORNING ROUTINE
- DAILY DRESS-UP
- MINDFUL MOVEMENT
- EAT YOUR VEGGIES
- JOURNAL
- GOAL REVIEW
- GRATITUDE
- EVENING ROUTINE

3
- MORNING ROUTINE
- DAILY DRESS-UP
- MINDFUL MOVEMENT
- EAT YOUR VEGGIES
- JOURNAL
- GOAL REVIEW
- GRATITUDE
- EVENING ROUTINE

4
- MORNING ROUTINE
- DAILY DRESS-UP
- MINDFUL MOVEMENT
- EAT YOUR VEGGIES
- JOURNAL
- GOAL REVIEW
- GRATITUDE
- EVENING ROUTINE

5
- MORNING ROUTINE
- DAILY DRESS-UP
- MINDFUL MOVEMENT
- EAT YOUR VEGGIES
- JOURNAL
- GOAL REVIEW
- GRATITUDE
- EVENING ROUTINE

6
- MORNING ROUTINE
- DAILY DRESS-UP
- MINDFUL MOVEMENT
- EAT YOUR VEGGIES
- JOURNAL
- GOAL REVIEW
- GRATITUDE
- EVENING ROUTINE

7
- MORNING ROUTINE
- DAILY DRESS-UP
- MINDFUL MOVEMENT
- EAT YOUR VEGGIES
- JOURNAL
- GOAL REVIEW
- GRATITUDE
- EVENING ROUTINE

8
- MORNING ROUTINE
- DAILY DRESS-UP
- MINDFUL MOVEMENT
- EAT YOUR VEGGIES
- JOURNAL
- GOAL REVIEW
- GRATITUDE
- EVENING ROUTINE

9
- MORNING ROUTINE
- DAILY DRESS-UP
- MINDFUL MOVEMENT
- EAT YOUR VEGGIES
- JOURNAL
- GOAL REVIEW
- GRATITUDE
- EVENING ROUTINE

10
- MORNING ROUTINE
- DAILY DRESS-UP
- MINDFUL MOVEMENT
- EAT YOUR VEGGIES
- JOURNAL
- GOAL REVIEW
- GRATITUDE
- EVENING ROUTINE

11
- MORNING ROUTINE
- DAILY DRESS-UP
- MINDFUL MOVEMENT
- EAT YOUR VEGGIES
- JOURNAL
- GOAL REVIEW
- GRATITUDE
- EVENING ROUTINE

12
- MORNING ROUTINE
- DAILY DRESS-UP
- MINDFUL MOVEMENT
- EAT YOUR VEGGIES
- JOURNAL
- GOAL REVIEW
- GRATITUDE
- EVENING ROUTINE

13
- MORNING ROUTINE
- DAILY DRESS-UP
- MINDFUL MOVEMENT
- EAT YOUR VEGGIES
- JOURNAL
- GOAL REVIEW
- GRATITUDE
- EVENING ROUTINE

14
- MORNING ROUTINE
- DAILY DRESS-UP
- MINDFUL MOVEMENT
- EAT YOUR VEGGIES
- JOURNAL
- GOAL REVIEW
- GRATITUDE
- EVENING ROUTINE

15
- MORNING ROUTINE
- DAILY DRESS-UP
- MINDFUL MOVEMENT
- EAT YOUR VEGGIES
- JOURNAL
- GOAL REVIEW
- GRATITUDE
- EVENING ROUTINE

16
- MORNING ROUTINE
- DAILY DRESS-UP
- MINDFUL MOVEMENT
- EAT YOUR VEGGIES
- JOURNAL
- GOAL REVIEW
- GRATITUDE
- EVENING ROUTINE

17
- MORNING ROUTINE
- DAILY DRESS-UP
- MINDFUL MOVEMENT
- EAT YOUR VEGGIES
- JOURNAL
- GOAL REVIEW
- GRATITUDE
- EVENING ROUTINE

18
- MORNING ROUTINE
- DAILY DRESS-UP
- MINDFUL MOVEMENT
- EAT YOUR VEGGIES
- JOURNAL
- GOAL REVIEW
- GRATITUDE
- EVENING ROUTINE

19
- MORNING ROUTINE
- DAILY DRESS-UP
- MINDFUL MOVEMENT
- EAT YOUR VEGGIES
- JOURNAL
- GOAL REVIEW
- GRATITUDE
- EVENING ROUTINE

20
- MORNING ROUTINE
- DAILY DRESS-UP
- MINDFUL MOVEMENT
- EAT YOUR VEGGIES
- JOURNAL
- GOAL REVIEW
- GRATITUDE
- EVENING ROUTINE

21
- MORNING ROUTINE
- DAILY DRESS-UP
- MINDFUL MOVEMENT
- EAT YOUR VEGGIES
- JOURNAL
- GOAL REVIEW
- GRATITUDE
- EVENING ROUTINE

22
- MORNING ROUTINE
- DAILY DRESS-UP
- MINDFUL MOVEMENT
- EAT YOUR VEGGIES
- JOURNAL
- GOAL REVIEW
- GRATITUDE
- EVENING ROUTINE

23
- MORNING ROUTINE
- DAILY DRESS-UP
- MINDFUL MOVEMENT
- EAT YOUR VEGGIES
- JOURNAL
- GOAL REVIEW
- GRATITUDE
- EVENING ROUTINE

24
- MORNING ROUTINE
- DAILY DRESS-UP
- MINDFUL MOVEMENT
- EAT YOUR VEGGIES
- JOURNAL
- GOAL REVIEW
- GRATITUDE
- EVENING ROUTINE

25
- MORNING ROUTINE
- DAILY DRESS-UP
- MINDFUL MOVEMENT
- EAT YOUR VEGGIES
- JOURNAL
- GOAL REVIEW
- GRATITUDE
- EVENING ROUTINE

26
- MORNING ROUTINE
- DAILY DRESS-UP
- MINDFUL MOVEMENT
- EAT YOUR VEGGIES
- JOURNAL
- GOAL REVIEW
- GRATITUDE
- EVENING ROUTINE

27
- MORNING ROUTINE
- DAILY DRESS-UP
- MINDFUL MOVEMENT
- EAT YOUR VEGGIES
- JOURNAL
- GOAL REVIEW
- GRATITUDE
- EVENING ROUTINE

28
- MORNING ROUTINE
- DAILY DRESS-UP
- MINDFUL MOVEMENT
- EAT YOUR VEGGIES
- JOURNAL
- GOAL REVIEW
- GRATITUDE
- EVENING ROUTINE

29
- MORNING ROUTINE
- DAILY DRESS-UP
- MINDFUL MOVEMENT
- EAT YOUR VEGGIES
- JOURNAL
- GOAL REVIEW
- GRATITUDE
- EVENING ROUTINE

30
- MORNING ROUTINE
- DAILY DRESS-UP
- MINDFUL MOVEMENT
- EAT YOUR VEGGIES
- JOURNAL
- GOAL REVIEW
- GRATITUDE
- EVENING ROUTINE

self-care

"CARING FOR MYSELF IS NOT SELF-INDULGENCE, IT IS SELF-PRESERVATION, AND THAT IS AN ACT OF POLITICAL WARFARE." —AUDRE LORDE

Nearly 20 years ago I read a quote by Julia Cameron in *The Artist's Way* that has stuck with me, "There is a connection between self-nurturing and self-respect."

It's easy to toss self-care aside as frivolous acts made up of only bubble baths and spa dates. Yet the practices run much deeper. Self-care encompasses all that we do to nourish our physical and mental health—behaviors, activities, and skills we use to take care of ourselves. Benefits of self-care include mental and physical health, increased self-knowledge, a chance to refocus, boosted immune system, and less susceptibility to stress, anxiety, and depression.

When I go through phases of feeling grumpy and out of sorts, I usually notice that my self-care practices have taken a back seat to the latest deadline or drama. Although that's just the first step, then I have to make changes to get back on track. As we know, that's the hard part.

In early 2018, my partner Tim and I drove halfway across the country to pick up our third rescue pug Gizmo as I was launching the *Year of Tranquility* online program. When back in DC with Gizmo, we immediately took him to our vet and found out he had cancerous mast cell tumors that required surgery.

Needless to say, the first few weeks were chaotic. Looking back I went into survival mode to get the program launched, Gizmo healed, and our household stabilized with the addition of a fourth pet.

It wasn't until later that month that I realized many of my go-tos had fallen to the wayside—mindful movement, restful sleep, journaling, AM/PM rituals. These practices keep me grounded and less reactionary. And, they're also the first to go when life gets away from me.

Once I realized what was happening, I penned a blog post about it that read:

While many wonderful things happened such as launching Year of Tranquility *and adopting Gizmo, it felt like I wasn't able to settle into the month. You know, like a snow globe all shaken up and instead of the flakes falling to the bottom, they continually swirl.*

Between Gizmo's cancer diagnosis and surgery, a 26-hour drive to and from St. Louis, a weekend jaunt to Seattle, assorted disappointments, and teaching multiple workshops and classes, my energy never quite recovered.

While musing in my journal last week, I realized I hadn't exercised in way too long and had been eating poorly. Duh, of course I was feeling yucky! That evening I carved out space for a yoga class and returned to more salads and smoothies. I won't say I'm 100 percent, but I am feeling better.

It seems that January can have that effect on many people. At times like this, it can be good to return to the basics. Are we eating right? Are we exercising? Are we sleeping? Are we hydrated? Yes, the very basics!

Recognizing that I felt out of sync and it was an easy enough fix—move and eat better—allowed me to course-correct and feel better immediately. It's the simple act of awareness. Notice when things feel off mentally, physically, and emotionally and then consider what you can do in that moment (short term) and moving forward (long term) to get back on track.

Sometimes this means a weekend getaway, a mental health day off from work, an afternoon retreat to a café with a novel, or a full-on day curled up in bed. Every few months I'll toss aside my to-dos and crawl under the covers to declare Bed Day. It's my form of waving a white flag. I'm cooked, possibly to a delicate crisp, and need to hit the reset button.

I'll gather soft linens, big bottle of water, a Do Not Disturb sign on the door, journal, pen, thermos of hot tea, and a pile of books. I've also been known to pull my mattress in front of the fireplace to have a full-fledged sensory experience. As we know, it's all about the details.

The term Bed Day came up over a decade ago when I would try to take Sundays off. Out of exhaustion, I would often stay in bed wearing whatever I'd slept in surrounded by my planner and laptop trying to sort out big picture problems.

Over the years I've realized that this is not the way to rest (yep, slow learner) and to save strategizing and brainstorming for when I'm feeling fresh and energized.

A Bed Day is your opportunity to put laundry, groceries, work, others' demands, and family obligations on hold while you rest and gain perspective—ultimately allowing you to be much more present for others and life's challenges.

We seem to find time to care for others and yet our needs may only get any time or energy that's left over. This month we'll explore the 15 practices listed on the self-care checklist (p. 157) and consider the role of self-care in daily life. Note what resonates and leave the rest. However, I strongly recommend you carve out at least 10 minutes per day to prioritize self-care.

Wellness educator Lalah Delia wrote, "Self-care is how you take your power back," and I have to agree. Self-care lets us get back in the driver seat of our lives.

savvy sources

BOOKS:
Self-Care for the Real World by Nadia Narain and Katia Phillips
The Book of Self-Care by Mary Beth Janssen
The Woman's Comfort Book by Jen Louden
Pretty Happy by Kate Hudson
A Book That Takes Its Time by Irene Smit and Astrid van der Hulst
Writing as a Way of Healing by Louise DeSalvo
Slow Beauty by Shel Pink

APPS:
Grid Diary
Food Monster

TRANQUILITY DU JOUR PODCASTS:
#61 Self-Nurturing Survival
#348 Mindful Self-Care
#370 Sipping Tea
#397 Nourish 360
#426 Breaking Up with Busy

1

WEEK 1: SLEEP, BATHE, BREATHE, MOVE

Although I offer 15 possible practices (p. 157) over these four weeks, ask yourself what self-care looks like to you. Note which of these practices you would like to spend more time cultivating. To make the time to focus on these practices, what would you need to let go of? Review your planner and look for ways to make these practices more of a priority.

RESTFUL SLEEP

Ariana Huffington, co-founder of *The Huffington Post*, is a big proponent of sleep. In her book *Thrive* she wrote, "Rob yourself of sleep and you'll find you do not function at your personal best. This is true of work decisions, relationship challenges, or any life situation that requires judgment, emotional equilibrium, problem solving, and creativity." To improve your sleep, go to bed earlier, avoid digital screens, keep your room dark and cool, limit that caffeine intake, and postpone worrying and brainstorming to a set time during the day. I keep a pen and paper by my bed to capture these random thoughts and then return to dreaming. Additional tools include fresh linens, soft blankets, weighted blankets, earplugs, eyepillows, and fans. For a dash of decadence, nap. Even 20 minutes can make you feel refreshed.

WARM BATH

A soak in the tub offers mental and physical benefits such as easing muscle aches, reducing pain and inflammation, and calming the nervous system. In ancient times, baths were thought to cure mental illness. Make it an experience—light a candle, read a magazine, listen to soothing music, add aromatherapy, bubbles, or almond oil. Feel the water on your skin.

DEEP BREATHING

Deep, full breathing is an important part of our self-care practice AND easy peasy to do in the moment. Each day, pause and take 5–10 deep breaths when you think of it. Breathe deeply when you're at a stoplight, stuck in traffic, on a tough call, in a frustrating meeting, soaking in the tub, having dinner with your family—truly anytime! Deep breathing helps with digestion, energy, and relaxation.

MINDFUL MOVEMENT

Stretch, swim, run, do yoga, dance, walk, bike, or whatever physical activity you enjoy. Strive for 10k steps each day. Avoid long periods of sitting without movement. Exercise regularly to help sleep better at night and feel more awake during the day. Movement releases endorphins and is good for your muscles, mind, and bones.

This week consider ways to incorporate these four practices into your daily life. Choose one that needs more attention and do it for 10 minutes every day.

weekly tranquility tools

- PLAN WEEK'S MITS
- PEN A LOVE NOTE
- SOAK IN THE TUB
- ARTIST DATE
- DIGITAL DAY OFF
- GREEN JUICE
- CLEAR CLUTTER
- BUY OR PICK FRESH FLOWERS

WEEK 2: JOURNALING, GRATITUDE, POSITIVE SELF-TALK, MINDFUL EATING

JOURNALING

Putting pen to paper (or fingers to keyboard) can be a therapeutic brain dump that also serves as a light into dark, unexplored places. Let your pen or hand dance freely across the page or keyboard. Make lists, create a mind map (a visual organization of information), answer a basic prompt that will change each time you write "At this moment I am feeling . . .," and process what emotions arise and why. After a few weeks, months, or years of doing this, you'll have lots of fodder for exploring and better understanding patterns, motivations, fears, and struggles. See Writing for more ideas.

GRATITUDE

Grab a paper and pen and take a moment to contemplate what you're grateful for right now. A cool or warm home, a simple joy, a romantic relationship, a pet, a family member, a comfy bed, a dear friend, a green juice, colored pencils, good health, mint tea, twinkle lights—you name it! Studies show that expressing gratitude can lower stress levels, improve sleep and self-esteem, enhance empathy, and increase perspective. Try a gratitude partner, someone to check in with regularly and share what you're grateful for.

SEEK BALANCE BETWEEN DOING AND BEING.

POSITIVE SELF-TALK

Try to eliminate internal negative chatter. Say "cancel, cancel" when those thoughts arise and reroute to the present moment or a pleasant memory. Express positive affirmations to yourself such as "you've got this" or "you're doing your best." Avoid saying anything to yourself that you wouldn't say to a dear friend. Take your stories to court. For example, do you know beyond a reasonable doubt that your boss is upset with you or that you're not getting better at a skill? No, you probably don't! Replace negative influences with positive ones—it rubs off on you. Shift self-talk from, "I have so much to do, I'm overwhelmed," to "I'm in charge of my life." Positive self-talk promotes hope, optimism, and happiness.

MINDFUL EATING

Mindful eating is the practice of noticing thoughts, feelings, and sensations while eating. Rather than consuming food unconsciously while watching TV or driving to work, mindful eating means savoring texture, smell, and taste with each bite. It's also a way to honor the farmer who grew the food, the sunshine and soil that gave the food fuel, the people who transported the food, and those who set it out at the farmers' market or grocery store. Try a meal in silence without doing anything else. Put your fork down between bites. Chew thoroughly. Listen to when your body is full (that can take 20 minutes, which is why slllooowwww is helpful here), and then stop. Mindful eating also helps us notice patterns—if we eat when sad, if we reach for sugar when tired, if we eat more when in social settings.

This week consider ways to incorporate these four practices into your daily life. Choose one that needs more attention and do it for 10 minutes every day.

weekly tranquility tools

- PLAN WEEK'S MITS
- SOAK IN THE TUB
- DIGITAL DAY OFF
- CLEAR CLUTTER
- PEN A LOVE NOTE
- ARTIST DATE
- GREEN JUICE
- BUY OR PICK FRESH FLOWERS

WEEK 3: GOALS, RITUALS, DIGITAL DOWN TIME, CREATIVE PLAY

GOAL REVIEW

Take a peek at the dreams and goals on your wish list regularly to stay in connection with the bigger picture. Each month I pen my "Month's Dreams" and, at the end of each month, I review them. These typically range from "release two podcasts" to "take 10 ballet classes" to "write blog post about X." If possible, I recommend reading over your Month's Dreams each day. This helps our daily decisions stay in alignment with the direction of our dreams. Plus, it's rewarding to watch and acknowledge our progress!

AM/PM RITUAL

Morning and evening rituals help reduce decision fatigue, help us stay grounded, and ensure the important things get done. These practices become bookends to the day. Greet your day with a yoga sun salutation, a cup of tea, writing time, or a brisk walk—starting with an intentional, tranquil tone. End your day with reflection. Shut down technology, soak in the tub, review tomorrow's agenda, or read in bed for 30 minutes before lights out. Your ritual could be five minutes or a few hours. Try it out and see what works best for you at this stage of life.

DIGITAL DOWN TIME

Our connection to technology needs the off switch from time to time. Whether it's checking social media, news, email, or surfing the internet, grant yourself a sabbatical from being glued to technology. To get started, disable those pesky push notifications, switch to airplane mode from time to time, buy an alarm clock versus using your phone, put devices away during meals or conversations, and/or ask yourself why when you reach for your phone.

CREATIVE PLAY

Think back to Creativity and the practices you dabbled in that month, from art journaling to hand lettering to trying a new form of movement. Creating provides a sense of completion and pride for bringing something new into the world. Although it can be hard to be a beginner (you should see my hand lettering!), it stimulates the brain and helps us grow. What are you curious about and interested in learning? Make a list of exhibits to see, crafts to learn, pieces to write, books to read, recipes to try, activities to do.

This week consider ways to incorporate these four practices into your daily life. Choose one that needs more attention and do it for 10 minutes every day.

weekly tranquility tools

- ○ PLAN WEEK'S MITS
- ○ PEN A LOVE NOTE
- ○ SOAK IN THE TUB
- ○ ARTIST DATE
- ○ DIGITAL DAY OFF
- ○ GREEN JUICE
- ○ CLEAR CLUTTER
- ○ BUY OR PICK FRESH FLOWERS

WEEK 4: MEDITATION, LOVING, HYDRATION

MEDITATION

Meditation is a practice of training the mind to focus while observing your thoughts without judgment. Sit still with a tall spine or lie down, close your eyes (if that's comfortable for you), and bring your attention to the breath moving in and out of your body. Try to begin or end your day with a minute of deep breathing while noticing your bodily sensations, thoughts, and feelings. Notice an increase in self-awareness and inner peace. More on this in Mindfulness.

LOVING CONNECTION

Spend time with those you love. If they're far away, call, text, or email them regularly. Make a date to have lunch or dinner with a friend. Reach out to someone you like but haven't seen in a while. Create a support system with those who share your interests and values. Join a support group for people who struggle with the same things you do. Try Gottman's Six Magic Hours. Refer back to Love for more ideas.

STAY HYDRATED

Drinking enough water helps energy levels, enhances mood and brain function, prevents headaches, helps to prevent kidney stones, and helps with weight loss (drinking water half an hour before meals can help you feel more full). The recommended amount is eight 8-ounce glasses and it can be helpful to track consumption or to make sure your reusable water bottle is refilled a certain number of times each day. Consider toting a water bottle with you everywhere you go. I even sleep with mine within reach—it's like my adult pacifier.

This week consider ways to incorporate these three practices into your daily life. Choose one that needs more attention and do it for 10 minutes every day.

weekly tranquility tools

- ○ PLAN WEEK'S MITS
- ○ PEN A LOVE NOTE
- ○ SOAK IN THE TUB
- ○ ARTIST DATE
- ○ DIGITAL DAY OFF
- ○ GREEN JUICE
- ○ CLEAR CLUTTER
- ○ BUY OR PICK FRESH FLOWERS

self-care checklist

TRACK YOUR DAILY USE OF THESE SELF-CARE PRACTICES FOR TWO WEEKS.

	1	2	3	4	5	6	7	8	9	10	11	12	13	14
RESTFUL SLEEP														
WARM BATH														
DEEP BREATHING														
MINDFUL MOVEMENT														
JOURNALING														
GRATITUDE														
POSTIVE SELF-TALK														
MINDFUL EATING														
GOAL REVIEW														
AM & PM RITUALS														
DIGITAL DOWN TIME														
CREATIVE PLAY														
MEDITATION														
LOVING CONNECTION														
STAY HYDRATED														

observations:

monthly planner

MONTH: _____   INTENTION: _____

SUNDAY	MONDAY	TUESDAY	WEDNESDAY	THURSDAY	FRIDAY	SATURDAY

monthly tranquility tools and practices

- ○ CRAFT MONTH'S DREAMS
- ○ REVIEW BUDGET
- ○ WEEK 1

- ○ CREATE SOMETHING
- ○ READ TWO BOOKS
- ○ WEEK 2

- ○ VOLUNTEER
- ○ MANI/PEDI
- ○ WEEK 3

- ○ ENTERTAIN
- ○ MASSAGE
- ○ WEEK 4

month's dreams

month's review

moon phases

Notice your connection to the moon's cycles in these four phases: *new, waxing, full, waning.* Consider the prompts below as a way to tie into your Month's Dreams and provide space for monthly reflection.

new moon

**A TIME FOR SETTING INTENTIONS.
I WANT...**

waxing moon

**A TIME FOR ACTION.
I WILL...**

full moon

**A TIME FOR HARVEST AND CLOSURE.
I RELEASE...**

waning moon

**A TIME FOR SOFTENING.
I FEEL...**

daily checklist

TRACK YOUR INCORPORATION OF THE DAILY TRANQUILITY TOOLS.

For each day (1–30), check off:
- ○ MORNING ROUTINE
- ○ DAILY DRESS-UP
- ○ MINDFUL MOVEMENT
- ○ EAT YOUR VEGGIES
- ○ JOURNAL
- ○ GOAL REVIEW
- ○ GRATITUDE
- ○ EVENING ROUTINE
- ○ _____

LESS IS MORE.

SIMPLIFY, SIMPLIFY.

mindfulness

"BETWEEN STIMULUS AND RESPONSE THERE IS SPACE. IN THAT SPACE IS OUR POWER TO CHOOSE OUR RESPONSE. IN OUR RESPONSE LIES OUR GROWTH AND OUR FREEDOM." —VICTOR FRANKL

O*ne sultry June a few summers ago, I sat at the feet of Jon Kabat-Zinn for seven days. Ready to drink up as much as possible from the mindfulness master, I joined 200 other mental health practitioners eager to incorporate mindfulness-based stress reduction into our practices. Since reading* Wherever You Go, There You Are *in my early days of teaching yoga, I've been deeply drawn to him and his work.*

Kabat-Zinn defines mindfulness as "paying attention in a particular way: on purpose, in the present moment, and nonjudgmentally." Instead of going down the rabbit hole with our thoughts (usually about the past or future), we make a conscious effort to catch ourselves and bring awareness back to the present moment.

After the first day of training on June 9, 2014, I wrote a blog post about the first three-hour lecture and shared this quote, "Real meditation practice is how you live your life—moment by moment by moment—whatever the circumstances you find yourself in." Mindfulness is a way of living, not just a practice of sitting still and breathing.

One of my biggest aha moments came years before after reading the above Viktor Frankl quote. It emphasizes that we have a choice in how we respond to life's challenges, whether it's an upsetting email, a loss, or a delayed flight.

Oftentimes we can feel that things are out of our control. However, we always have a choice in how to respond. And, as the quote reminds us, it's between the stimulus (trigger) and response that our freedom is found.

It's our freedom to choose. In theory, this is simple. In practice, it takes work to carve those new neuropathways and shift our automatic reactions.

This month we'll explore an array of formal mindfulness practices such as a mindful check-in, walking meditation, seated meditation, body-scan, mindful breathing, and loving-kindness meditation.

We'll also touch on informal practices such as mindful eating, practicing STOP, mindful communication, journaling, and mindful moments.

Benefits of mindfulness include an increase in acceptance, compassion, concentration, and self-control, along with a decrease in stress (to name a few). Neuroscientists have found that after just 11 hours of meditation, practitioners had structural changes in the part of the brain involved in monitoring our focus and self-control.

Ultimately, mindfulness is the process of deep awareness and accepting each experience, each sensation, thought, or feeling, just as it is, without trying to change it.

I use it as a practice to better understand my triggers and myself. Hmmm, why does that email bother me so much? What about that comment upset me? Why do I feel sick to my belly when I think about X? Rather than an immediate reaction, it's helpful to notice what we're experiencing, name it, and then navigate the situation with better understanding.

Emotions are like weather patterns that change and pass. Even when we're experiencing sadness, anxiety, or rage, if we give these feelings space, they will gradually diminish. Consider Pema Chödrön's wisdom, "You are the sky. Everything else is just the weather."

Mindfulness helps us live with more ease and tranquility. My wish is that these practices deepen connections, increase acceptance, and offer a sense of inner peace.

savvy sources

BOOKS:

Mindfulness-Based Stress Reduction Workbook by Bob Stahl and Elisha Goldstein
Full Catastrophe Living by Jon Kabat-Zinn
Wherever You Go, There You Are by Jon Kabat-Zinn
The Wisdom of No Escape by Pema Chodren
Real Happiness and *Real Happiness at Work* by Sharon Salzberg
Savor and *Peace Is Every Step* by Thich Nhat Hahn

APPS:

Headspace
Calm

TRANQUILITY DU JOUR PODCASTS:

#171 Musings on Mindfulness
#267 Mindfulness with Elisha Goldstein
#317 Mindfulness Diaries
#320 Mindfulness
#341 Everyday Mindfulness
#356 Uncovering Happiness
#357 Mindful Eating
#416 All Our Waves Are Water

1

WEEK 1: MINDFUL CHECK-IN, BODY SCAN, 10 MINDFUL MINUTES

MINDFUL CHECK-IN

A mindful check-in is a brief one- to three-minute pause in your day to notice how you're feeling physically, mentally, and emotionally in that moment. It can be done on the bus, at a stop light, in a meeting, or anywhere in between.

Begin by bringing awareness to your physical body, notice heat, coolness, tightness, and openness. Observe your emotions and name them. Notice your thoughts. Are they in the present moment, planning the future, or replaying something from the past? That's all there is to it!

BODY SCAN

Martha Graham says, "The body says what words cannot." To access the body, try a body scan—an investigation of physical sensations, thoughts, and emotions, typically done while lying down in a relaxed setting without distractions. Walk yourself through each part of your body starting with the toes to the hips to the fingertips to the top of the head.

Grab popcorn and watch Headspace's Andy Puddicombe's TED Talk about 10 mindful minutes.

This week try a mindful check-in daily and a body scan at least once. Practice being still, breathing, and observing your thoughts for 10 minutes each day.

weekly tranquility tools

- ○ PLAN WEEK'S MITS
- ○ PEN A LOVE NOTE
- ○ SOAK IN THE TUB
- ○ ARTIST DATE
- ○ DIGITAL DAY OFF
- ○ GREEN JUICE
- ○ CLEAR CLUTTER
- ○ BUY OR PICK FRESH FLOWERS

WEEK 2: SEATED AND WALKING MEDITATION

If you were to attend a silent meditation retreat, the facilitator typically would alternate between seated and walking meditation throughout the journey. This gives your body a chance to balance movement and stillness while staying present.

SEATED MEDITATION

Come to a comfortable seated position. Close your eyes and pay attention to your breath, body, thoughts, and emotions. As your mind wanders, bring it back to the breath to build concentration, observe your emotions, and notice physical sensations like clenching of the jaw. You will get distracted repeatedly and it doesn't mean you're doing it wrong. The act of noticing you're distracted and returning to your breath IS the practice of meditation. Stay here for two to 10 minutes.

WALKING MEDITATION

Instead of getting from point A to point B, the point of walking meditation is to arrive in the present moment of each step. Notice the movement of each foot as you lift it, move it forward, and place it back down with each step. Lift, shift, place. Walk back and forth in a line at home or wander on a large lawn. Practice for five to 10 minutes.

This week keep up the practice of being still, breathing, and observing your thoughts. Try walking meditation once this week for 15 minutes and note what comes up for you.

weekly tranquility tools

- ○ PLAN WEEK'S MITS
- ○ PEN A LOVE NOTE
- ○ SOAK IN THE TUB
- ○ ARTIST DATE
- ○ DIGITAL DAY OFF
- ○ GREEN JUICE
- ○ CLEAR CLUTTER
- ○ BUY OR PICK FRESH FLOWERS

WEEK 3: STOP AND MINDFUL EATING

STOP

S: Stop
T: Take a breath
O: Observe what's happening
P: Proceed with awareness

Throughout the day as I find myself triggered by a comment, upsetting news, overwhelm, or anything in between, I keep STOP in mind. It's a great tool to help recenter and reconnect in the moment. I try to pause, observe my breath, and notice what's going on with me mentally, physically, and emotionally (similar to a mindful check-in). Then I strive to proceed with responding versus reacting.

Remember Viktor Frankl's quote, "Between stimulus and response there is a space. In that space is our power to choose our response. In our response lies our growth and our freedom." Well, the practice of STOP allows us to make that space and, ideally, experience more freedom without being bound by our habitual patterning. Good stuff!

MINDFUL EATING (AND DRINKING)

Mindful eating is detailed in Self-Care, so let's chat mindful drinking. Vietnamese Buddhist monk and peace activist Thich Nhat Hanh encourages us to, "Drink your tea slowly and reverently, as if it is the axis on which the world revolves—slowly, evenly, without rushing toward the future. Live the actual moment. Only this moment is life." Tea sipping has been a daily habit (some would say obsession) of mine for years. I even travel with my favorite tea bags to avoid those disappointing moments when I order a green tea and am told, "I'm sorry, we only have Lipton."

Tea or coffee drinking can become a sacred ritual to start and/or end your day. And, of course, to savor anytime in between. Begin by setting an intention for the day or for that moment. Heat the water and listen to it boil. Choose your tea type. Pour the water over your tea and listen to it flow into your mug. After letting it steep two to five minutes, wrap your hands around the warm cup and take in the aroma. Notice the steam rising and take a sip. Follow it as it slides down your throat.

This week keep up the practice of being still, breathing, and observing your thoughts for 10 minutes each day. When you find yourself feeling triggered, try STOP. Eat and drink with attention.

weekly tranquility tools

- ○ PLAN WEEK'S MITS
- ○ PEN A LOVE NOTE
- ○ SOAK IN THE TUB
- ○ ARTIST DATE
- ○ DIGITAL DAY OFF
- ○ GREEN JUICE
- ○ CLEAR CLUTTER
- ○ BUY OR PICK FRESH FLOWERS

WEEK 4: MINDFUL COMMUNICATION

Mindful communication is listening and speaking with compassion, kindness, and awareness. It involves considering what we bring to the communication, rather than what we can get from it.

A student asked Buddhist scholar Robert Thurman how to practice mindfulness most effectively. He suggested getting a cup of coffee from the corner deli and elaborated, "The guy in the deli doesn't have a very exciting job. He's not well paid and people give him a hard time all day. How do you treat him? Are you kind? Are you impatient? Do you ask how his day is going?"

This is mindfulness practice—the nitty-gritty mechanics of daily life. How we act is a reflection of what we think and how we feel.

MINDFUL LISTENING

- Remove distractions and set the space to be fully present.
- Set an intention to receive what they are saying without hearing blame or criticism.
- Pay attention to your physical sensations, thoughts, and emotions.
- When unclear, ask, "What I hear you saying is X. Is that correct?"
- Avoid judgment, maintain eye contact, and forgo interrupting.

MINDFUL SPEAKING

- Use the acronym WAIT (Why Am I Talking?) and asking yourself: Is it true? Is it kind? Is it necessary?
- Speak with intention and practice being clear, concise, and compassionate.
- Stay mindful of your tone, volume, and body language.
- Take a pause and breathe before speaking.
- Ask, "How can I support you?"
- Use "I" statements.
- Notice physical sensations, thoughts, and emotions.

This week practice mindful communication when interacting with someone you love and/or who triggers you.

weekly tranquility tools

- PLAN WEEK'S MITS
- PEN A LOVE NOTE
- SOAK IN THE TUB
- ARTIST DATE
- DIGITAL DAY OFF
- GREEN JUICE
- CLEAR CLUTTER
- BUY OR PICK FRESH FLOWERS

everyday mindfulness

TAKE A BATH AND FEEL THE WATER ON YOUR SKIN. LISTEN TO MUSIC AND LET IT WASH OVER YOU (TRY BOLERO). WASH THE DISHES AND NOTICE THE SUDS. SIP YOUR MORNING TEA AND NOTICE THE SENSATION AS IT SLIDES DOWN YOUR THROAT. LET A PIECE OF DARK CHOCOLATE MELT IN YOUR MOUTH. LISTEN FULLY TO THE PERSON IN FRONT OF YOU. LAUGH AND FEEL YOUR BELLY MOVE. GO TO A MOVEMENT CLASS AND PAY ATTENTION TO THE SENSATIONS IN YOUR BODY. SLIP INTO YOUR CLOTHING AND NOTICE HOW IT FEELS AGAINST YOUR SKIN. EAT A MEAL IN SILENCE. CREATE A TO-DO LIST USING HAND LETTERING AND NOTICE THE MOVEMENTS OF THE PEN. VISIT A MUSEUM AND OBSERVE THE BRUSH STROKES IN A PAINTING. GO ON A WALK AND NOTICE THE FLORA AND FAUNA. BAKE SCONES AND FEEL YOUR HANDS KNEADING THE DOUGH. SAVOR THE SMELL OF FRESHLY-BAKED COOKIES STRAIGHT FROM THE OVEN. TEND TO YOUR PLANTS AND REMOVE DEAD LEAVES. WRITE IN YOUR JOURNAL AND FEEL THE PEN MOVE ACROSS THE PAGE AND THE EMOTIONS THAT ARISE. NOTICE AND NAME YOUR FEELINGS. SPEND TIME IN NATURE AND NOTICE THE SMELLS AND SOUNDS.

seasonal life review

DATE: _____

SEASONALLY REFLECT ON AREAS OF YOUR LIFE. RATE EACH ONE WITH YOUR LEVEL OF SATISFACTION 10 = BLISS, 5 = SO-SO, 0 = BOO.

Here are some additional areas to consider: social life, romance, family, education, health, fitness, meaning, activism. Next, take a moment to note the areas that ranked low and create three action steps to increase your tranquility in these areas. Be gentle. Plant seeds. Watch dreams take root.

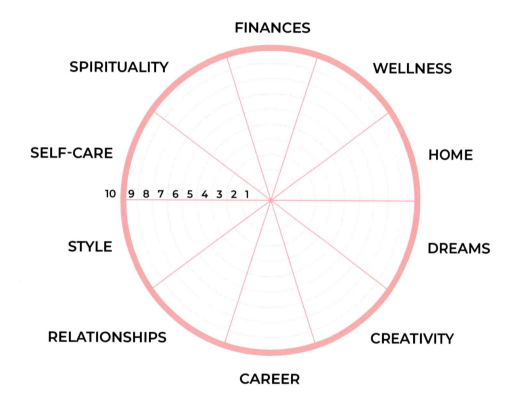

ACTION STEPS TO INCREASE AREAS THAT ARE LOWER THAN I'D LIKE:

seasonal checklist

- ○ WHEEL OF LIFE
- ○ DEEP CLEAN
- ○ PRACTICE ESSENTIALISM
- ○ TRY SOMETHING NEW
- ○ BED DAY
- ○ REARRANGE
- ○ GET CULTURED
- ○ TEND YOUR GARDEN
- ○ _____

monthly planner

MONTH: _____   INTENTION: _____

SUNDAY	MONDAY	TUESDAY	WEDNESDAY	THURSDAY	FRIDAY	SATURDAY

monthly tranquility tools and practices

- ○ CRAFT MONTH'S DREAMS
- ○ REVIEW BUDGET
- ○ WEEK 1

- ○ CREATE SOMETHING
- ○ READ TWO BOOKS
- ○ WEEK 2

- ○ VOLUNTEER
- ○ MANI/PEDI
- ○ WEEK 3

- ○ ENTERTAIN
- ○ MASSAGE
- ○ WEEK 4

month's dreams

month's review

moon phases

Notice your connection to the moon's cycles in these four phases: new, waxing, full, waning. Consider the prompts below as a way to tie into your Month's Dreams and provide space for monthly reflection.

new moon

A TIME FOR SETTING INTENTIONS.
I WANT...

waxing moon

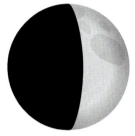

A TIME FOR ACTION.
I WILL...

full moon

A TIME FOR HARVEST AND CLOSURE.
I RELEASE...

waning moon

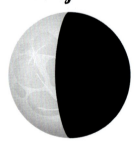

A TIME FOR SOFTENING.
I FEEL...

daily checklist

TRACK YOUR INCORPORATION OF THE DAILY TRANQUILITY TOOLS.

1
- [ ] MORNING ROUTINE
- [ ] DAILY DRESS-UP
- [ ] MINDFUL MOVEMENT
- [ ] EAT YOUR VEGGIES
- [ ] JOURNAL
- [ ] GOAL REVIEW
- [ ] GRATITUDE
- [ ] EVENING ROUTINE
- [ ] ____________________

2
- [ ] MORNING ROUTINE
- [ ] DAILY DRESS-UP
- [ ] MINDFUL MOVEMENT
- [ ] EAT YOUR VEGGIES
- [ ] JOURNAL
- [ ] GOAL REVIEW
- [ ] GRATITUDE
- [ ] EVENING ROUTINE
- [ ] ____________________

3
- [ ] MORNING ROUTINE
- [ ] DAILY DRESS-UP
- [ ] MINDFUL MOVEMENT
- [ ] EAT YOUR VEGGIES
- [ ] JOURNAL
- [ ] GOAL REVIEW
- [ ] GRATITUDE
- [ ] EVENING ROUTINE
- [ ] ____________________

4
- [ ] MORNING ROUTINE
- [ ] DAILY DRESS-UP
- [ ] MINDFUL MOVEMENT
- [ ] EAT YOUR VEGGIES
- [ ] JOURNAL
- [ ] GOAL REVIEW
- [ ] GRATITUDE
- [ ] EVENING ROUTINE
- [ ] ____________________

5
- [ ] MORNING ROUTINE
- [ ] DAILY DRESS-UP
- [ ] MINDFUL MOVEMENT
- [ ] EAT YOUR VEGGIES
- [ ] JOURNAL
- [ ] GOAL REVIEW
- [ ] GRATITUDE
- [ ] EVENING ROUTINE
- [ ] ____________________

6
- [ ] MORNING ROUTINE
- [ ] DAILY DRESS-UP
- [ ] MINDFUL MOVEMENT
- [ ] EAT YOUR VEGGIES
- [ ] JOURNAL
- [ ] GOAL REVIEW
- [ ] GRATITUDE
- [ ] EVENING ROUTINE
- [ ] ____________________

7
- [ ] MORNING ROUTINE
- [ ] DAILY DRESS-UP
- [ ] MINDFUL MOVEMENT
- [ ] EAT YOUR VEGGIES
- [ ] JOURNAL
- [ ] GOAL REVIEW
- [ ] GRATITUDE
- [ ] EVENING ROUTINE
- [ ] ____________________

8
- [ ] MORNING ROUTINE
- [ ] DAILY DRESS-UP
- [ ] MINDFUL MOVEMENT
- [ ] EAT YOUR VEGGIES
- [ ] JOURNAL
- [ ] GOAL REVIEW
- [ ] GRATITUDE
- [ ] EVENING ROUTINE
- [ ] ____________________

9
- [ ] MORNING ROUTINE
- [ ] DAILY DRESS-UP
- [ ] MINDFUL MOVEMENT
- [ ] EAT YOUR VEGGIES
- [ ] JOURNAL
- [ ] GOAL REVIEW
- [ ] GRATITUDE
- [ ] EVENING ROUTINE
- [ ] ____________________

10
- [ ] MORNING ROUTINE
- [ ] DAILY DRESS-UP
- [ ] MINDFUL MOVEMENT
- [ ] EAT YOUR VEGGIES
- [ ] JOURNAL
- [ ] GOAL REVIEW
- [ ] GRATITUDE
- [ ] EVENING ROUTINE
- [ ] ____________________

11
- [ ] MORNING ROUTINE
- [ ] DAILY DRESS-UP
- [ ] MINDFUL MOVEMENT
- [ ] EAT YOUR VEGGIES
- [ ] JOURNAL
- [ ] GOAL REVIEW
- [ ] GRATITUDE
- [ ] EVENING ROUTINE
- [ ] ____________________

12
- [ ] MORNING ROUTINE
- [ ] DAILY DRESS-UP
- [ ] MINDFUL MOVEMENT
- [ ] EAT YOUR VEGGIES
- [ ] JOURNAL
- [ ] GOAL REVIEW
- [ ] GRATITUDE
- [ ] EVENING ROUTINE
- [ ] ____________________

13
- [ ] MORNING ROUTINE
- [ ] DAILY DRESS-UP
- [ ] MINDFUL MOVEMENT
- [ ] EAT YOUR VEGGIES
- [ ] JOURNAL
- [ ] GOAL REVIEW
- [ ] GRATITUDE
- [ ] EVENING ROUTINE
- [ ] ____________________

14
- [ ] MORNING ROUTINE
- [ ] DAILY DRESS-UP
- [ ] MINDFUL MOVEMENT
- [ ] EAT YOUR VEGGIES
- [ ] JOURNAL
- [ ] GOAL REVIEW
- [ ] GRATITUDE
- [ ] EVENING ROUTINE
- [ ] ____________________

15
- [ ] MORNING ROUTINE
- [ ] DAILY DRESS-UP
- [ ] MINDFUL MOVEMENT
- [ ] EAT YOUR VEGGIES
- [ ] JOURNAL
- [ ] GOAL REVIEW
- [ ] GRATITUDE
- [ ] EVENING ROUTINE
- [ ] ____________________

16
- [ ] MORNING ROUTINE
- [ ] DAILY DRESS-UP
- [ ] MINDFUL MOVEMENT
- [ ] EAT YOUR VEGGIES
- [ ] JOURNAL
- [ ] GOAL REVIEW
- [ ] GRATITUDE
- [ ] EVENING ROUTINE
- [ ] ____________________

17
- [ ] MORNING ROUTINE
- [ ] DAILY DRESS-UP
- [ ] MINDFUL MOVEMENT
- [ ] EAT YOUR VEGGIES
- [ ] JOURNAL
- [ ] GOAL REVIEW
- [ ] GRATITUDE
- [ ] EVENING ROUTINE
- [ ] ____________________

18
- [ ] MORNING ROUTINE
- [ ] DAILY DRESS-UP
- [ ] MINDFUL MOVEMENT
- [ ] EAT YOUR VEGGIES
- [ ] JOURNAL
- [ ] GOAL REVIEW
- [ ] GRATITUDE
- [ ] EVENING ROUTINE
- [ ] ____________________

19
- [ ] MORNING ROUTINE
- [ ] DAILY DRESS-UP
- [ ] MINDFUL MOVEMENT
- [ ] EAT YOUR VEGGIES
- [ ] JOURNAL
- [ ] GOAL REVIEW
- [ ] GRATITUDE
- [ ] EVENING ROUTINE
- [ ] ____________________

20
- [ ] MORNING ROUTINE
- [ ] DAILY DRESS-UP
- [ ] MINDFUL MOVEMENT
- [ ] EAT YOUR VEGGIES
- [ ] JOURNAL
- [ ] GOAL REVIEW
- [ ] GRATITUDE
- [ ] EVENING ROUTINE
- [ ] ____________________

21
- [ ] MORNING ROUTINE
- [ ] DAILY DRESS-UP
- [ ] MINDFUL MOVEMENT
- [ ] EAT YOUR VEGGIES
- [ ] JOURNAL
- [ ] GOAL REVIEW
- [ ] GRATITUDE
- [ ] EVENING ROUTINE
- [ ] ____________________

22
- [ ] MORNING ROUTINE
- [ ] DAILY DRESS-UP
- [ ] MINDFUL MOVEMENT
- [ ] EAT YOUR VEGGIES
- [ ] JOURNAL
- [ ] GOAL REVIEW
- [ ] GRATITUDE
- [ ] EVENING ROUTINE
- [ ] ____________________

23
- [ ] MORNING ROUTINE
- [ ] DAILY DRESS-UP
- [ ] MINDFUL MOVEMENT
- [ ] EAT YOUR VEGGIES
- [ ] JOURNAL
- [ ] GOAL REVIEW
- [ ] GRATITUDE
- [ ] EVENING ROUTINE
- [ ] ____________________

24
- [ ] MORNING ROUTINE
- [ ] DAILY DRESS-UP
- [ ] MINDFUL MOVEMENT
- [ ] EAT YOUR VEGGIES
- [ ] JOURNAL
- [ ] GOAL REVIEW
- [ ] GRATITUDE
- [ ] EVENING ROUTINE
- [ ] ____________________

25
- [ ] MORNING ROUTINE
- [ ] DAILY DRESS-UP
- [ ] MINDFUL MOVEMENT
- [ ] EAT YOUR VEGGIES
- [ ] JOURNAL
- [ ] GOAL REVIEW
- [ ] GRATITUDE
- [ ] EVENING ROUTINE
- [ ] ____________________

26
- [ ] MORNING ROUTINE
- [ ] DAILY DRESS-UP
- [ ] MINDFUL MOVEMENT
- [ ] EAT YOUR VEGGIES
- [ ] JOURNAL
- [ ] GOAL REVIEW
- [ ] GRATITUDE
- [ ] EVENING ROUTINE
- [ ] ____________________

27
- [ ] MORNING ROUTINE
- [ ] DAILY DRESS-UP
- [ ] MINDFUL MOVEMENT
- [ ] EAT YOUR VEGGIES
- [ ] JOURNAL
- [ ] GOAL REVIEW
- [ ] GRATITUDE
- [ ] EVENING ROUTINE
- [ ] ____________________

28
- [ ] MORNING ROUTINE
- [ ] DAILY DRESS-UP
- [ ] MINDFUL MOVEMENT
- [ ] EAT YOUR VEGGIES
- [ ] JOURNAL
- [ ] GOAL REVIEW
- [ ] GRATITUDE
- [ ] EVENING ROUTINE
- [ ] ____________________

29
- [ ] MORNING ROUTINE
- [ ] DAILY DRESS-UP
- [ ] MINDFUL MOVEMENT
- [ ] EAT YOUR VEGGIES
- [ ] JOURNAL
- [ ] GOAL REVIEW
- [ ] GRATITUDE
- [ ] EVENING ROUTINE
- [ ] ____________________

30
- [ ] MORNING ROUTINE
- [ ] DAILY DRESS-UP
- [ ] MINDFUL MOVEMENT
- [ ] EAT YOUR VEGGIES
- [ ] JOURNAL
- [ ] GOAL REVIEW
- [ ] GRATITUDE
- [ ] EVENING ROUTINE
- [ ] ____________________

writing

"WE WRITE TO TASTE LIFE TWICE, IN THE MOMENT AND IN RETROSPECT." — ANAÏS NIN

*S*itting on the floor of my floral print-infused living room, I turned to a teacher participating in my first Artist's Way women's group and said, *"I want to write a book!"*

"Great, about what?"

That's where I stopped; I had no idea.

After some back and forth, we came to an agreement to trade yoga in exchange for writing coaching. She brought her Georgetown University syllabus to our first session and I realized that I was very, very lucky.

Two exercises that stick out from that experience include creating a vision/inspiration board and going to a bookstore.

When stumped with what I wanted to write about, my teacher had me pull images from magazines that represented what I wanted in my book. After scouring various images, I settled on those of happy couples, zen settings, yoga, bubble baths, nature, and healthy food.

One rainy weekday morning I met her at a Barnes & Noble in Georgetown to look for "book cousins." These are books similar to what I wanted to write. We noted where they were shelved, who wrote them, who their agents were (found in the Acknowledgements section), and what was missing from that genre.

This was 2001 and there were only a smattering of yoga books—mainly philosophy driven such as the *Bhagavad Gita*—and it covered one third of a tucked away shelf on the bookstore's second floor.

After the vision board and bookstore tour, I realized that there was a need for a yoga lifestyle book. *Sex and the City* and chick lit were popular at the time, so a playful, female-focused yoga-centric book felt like a perfect melding.

And that's how my first book, *Hip Tranquil Chick*, was born.

Since childhood I've written in a journal and this tool is like a therapist-to-go. After a few minutes of writing, I typically feel heard, seen, and am ready to move on. Not that I've let the challenge go, but it is no longer on repeat in my mind. I've given it room to breathe outside of my head.

We are all writers. We write emails, texts, letters, briefs, essays, poetry, short stories, novels, creative nonfiction, and recipes. There's no way around it, YOU are a writer!

This month we'll be exploring various practices, prompts, and more associated with writing. Since 2001, I've been studying the writing practice and over the past many years have attended numerous conferences, writing retreats, workshops, and read tons of writing books. In addition, I've been teaching about writing for over a decade and I have so much I'm excited to share with you!

Here are a few of my favorite tips to enhance your writing skills and they work with fiction, creative non-fiction, journaling, letters, and even email:

- Study writers whose voices you admire. Handwrite pages from their work to study their cadence, language, pacing, and sentence structure.
- Read, read, read. This is a non-negotiable and, well, it's a fun perk!
- Mind map your story or project.
- Start a blog to create a consistent practice.
- Collage what you want to write about to get clear on your reader, topics, and overarching theme.
- Start or join a supportive writing group.
- Visit a bookstore and notice which books and magazines you're drawn to. Note what's missing from your favorite genre or which editors and agentss (they're noted in the Acknowledgments section) you'd like to work with.
- Review the submission guidelines in magazines.
- Add dialogue to bring the characters and story to life.
- Include senses: sight, hearing, sound, touch (temperature and texture), taste.
- Create a powerful opening that evokes feelings, makes the conflict apparent, and leaves readers intrigued with questions about what's going to happen next.

In *The Writing Life*, Annie Dillard writes, "Write as if you were dying. At the same time, assume you write for an audience consisting solely of terminal patients. That is, after all, the case. What would you begin writing if you knew you would die soon?"

She also wrote, "How we spend our days is, of course, how we spend our lives."

Writing is a personal practice. A chance to bare our souls. An opportunity to give voice to our stories. A space to let our imagination run free. And so much more.

Wherever you are on the writing spectrum (from letters to publication), you are a writer with words to share. William Wordsworth wrote,

"Fill your paper with the breathings of your heart." Now, let THAT be our intention for this month together!

Savvy Sources

BOOKS:

Crafting the Personal Essay by Dinty Moore
Writing Tools by Roy Peter Clark
How the Light Gets In by Pat Schneider
Opening Up By Writing It Down by James Pennebaker and Joshua Smyth
The Art of Slow Writing by Louise DeSalvo
Writing Tools by Roy Peter Clark
On Writing Well by William Zinsser
Brevity: A Journal of Concise Literary Nonfiction (brevitymag.com)

APPS:

Mindly
Hemingway

TRANQUILITY DU JOUR PODCASTS:

#20 Journal Writing 101
#33 Book Writing 101
#96 The Writing Life
#142 Musing on Journal Writing
#222 Mind mapping
#337 Writing + Yoga
#363 The Writing Habit
#369 The Writing Practice
#407 The Writing Process

1
WEEK 1: JOURNAL WRITING

This may be a practice that you've done since grade school where you wrote about your crush of the day, a practice you pick up when you're upset and need a space to process, or something you've never done or understood. No matter how much journal writing you've done, my hope is that this will be a helpful gateway to engage with the experience.

Journal writing is the process of putting pen to paper (or fingers to keyboard) and, for many, it can be a therapeutic brain dump to bring light to dark, unchartered territory. As Joyce Chapman says in *Journaling for Joy*, "Through the act of writing things down, you allow yourself to wake up, be aware, and pay attention to what your life has to teach you."

IDEAS TO GET YOU STARTED:

1. Answer a basic prompt that will change each time you write, "At this moment I'm feeling . . ."
2. Write an unsent letter—to someone who's hurt you, whom you've hurt, who's passed away.
3. Capture your nighttime dreams.
4. Answer, "What question do I need to answer for myself? What do I want to know? What information do I need to tap into? What would I most like to get out of this writing?"
5. Answer, "Where am I in my life right now and where do I want to be?"
6. Explore an issue or experience from the third person or another person's point of view.

Journaling is a tool to help explore and better understand patterns, motivations, fears, and struggles. It's also a safe space to capture dreams, to celebrate, and to grow. Let's get started!

This week spend 10 minutes each day writing in a journal using one the suggested prompts.

weekly tranquility tools

- ○ PLAN WEEK'S MITS
- ○ PEN A LOVE NOTE
- ○ SOAK IN THE TUB
- ○ ARTIST DATE
- ○ DIGITAL DAY OFF
- ○ GREEN JUICE
- ○ CLEAR CLUTTER
- ○ BUY OR PICK FRESH FLOWERS

WEEK 2: THE POWER OF LISTS

Many of you are probably familiar with a to-do list, yet there are many other lists that we can write and create.

List making helps to curb that anxious, overwhelmed feeling of too much swimming around in our heads. Studies show that imagery is useful for people with anxiety, so making your lists beautiful can alleviate some of those anxious feelings swirling around.

It can also serve as a space of creativity. When making our lists with color and design like hand lettering and flourishes, we bring a creative streak into our everyday experience. Just search "bullet journaling lists" and you'll be filled with inspiration.

Rather than the typical ballpoint pen on lined paper or digital list, make it colorful, add doodles or flourishes, or write on a beautiful image pulled from a magazine. In other words, make it uniquely you.

Below you'll find an assortment of list ideas to get you started:

Worry, excited about, gratitude, want to do, bucket, dreams, today's accomplishments, ideal day, morning ritual, evening ritual, holiday gift list, holiday menus, birthdays and anniversaries, journaling prompts, food diary, current projects, meeting notes, exercise log, grocery, meal planning, recipes to try, movies to watch, books to read, restaurants to try, wishes, seasonal bucket, places to visit, fitness goals, mood tracker, things I love, favorite quotes, memories, blog posts to write, videos to shoot, things to photograph, monthly budget, items to buy, reading log, playlists, date ideas, outdoor activity ideas, causes you care about, blogs to follow, favorite Instagram accounts, packing lists, day trip ideas, job application log, essential oil recipes, beauty routine, self-care, relationship wishes, career wishes, habit tracker, pet care, child care, personal care, Q4 wish list, garden care, to be, home care.

weekly tranquility tools

- ○ PLAN WEEK'S MITS
- ○ PEN A LOVE NOTE
- ○ SOAK IN THE TUB
- ○ ARTIST DATE
- ○ DIGITAL DAY OFF
- ○ GREEN JUICE
- ○ CLEAR CLUTTER
- ○ BUY OR PICK FRESH FLOWERS

WHAT I DO AND SAY HAS A **RIPPLE EFFECT.**

WEEK 3: SNAIL MAIL

Sure, email is super efficient, but isn't it delightful to find a note with your name and address handwritten in the mailbox?

Snail mail is a form of slow writing where tender care is poured into the experience. From the stationery, to the envelope, to the stamp (it's like choosing my stamp design at USPS is a major life decision), to the way it's sealed (e.g., washi tape, wax seal, wafer seal, stickers), to what's tucked inside (e.g., article, tea bag, pressed flower, ephemera), to the way your name and address are written, to the message inside, to the pen you used—that's A LOT of personalization. Same goes for a postcard.

The sweet thing about letter writing is that it's a private exchange unlike updating a public forum like social media.

Snail mail is a snapshot in time, an artifact of sorts noting where you are, what you're thinking about, and what's going on for you.

You can incorporate the senses unlike in a digital format—tuck a tea bag inside (taste), use luxe paper (touch), write with a pink pen (sight), spritz with lavender spray (smell).

Plus, you can practice your hand lettering, calligraphy, or handwriting.

Writing and reading letters allows us to pause, slow down, and pay attention. Letter writing encourages us to choose our words carefully and concisely versus typing out a quick "thinking of you" text or email. Handwriting slows down the mind, and we become more present.

Do you feel inspired to pen a handwritten note of love, encouragement, affection, gratitude, inspiration, or anything in between? I sure hope so!

Pen a letter or postcard and send it via snail mail. Make someone's day.

weekly tranquility tools

- PLAN WEEK'S MITS
- PEN A LOVE NOTE
- SOAK IN THE TUB
- ARTIST DATE
- DIGITAL DAY OFF
- GREEN JUICE
- CLEAR CLUTTER
- BUY OR PICK FRESH FLOWERS

4
WEEK 4: MICRO-MEMOIR

A memoir is a sliver of your life while a micro-memoir is a peek into a moment. This genre engages readers at an emotional level and helps the reader come away with insight into the human condition.

According to Writer Mag, "The micro-memoir strives to combine the extreme abbreviation of poetry, the narrative tension of fiction, and the truth-telling of creative nonfiction. At its most basic, a micro-memoir is written in sentences, drawn from personal experience, and strives to create a world in as few words as possible."

These standalone pieces are powerful for the writer to give voice to their experiences and the reader gets to join the adventure.

To write a micro-memoir, list your defining moments (you know, that day when something changed—a phone call, a kiss, a job offer) and choose one that's calling to you to explore. Next, spend time writing about what that moment means to you now and start a draft of the moment choosing a word limit such as 500–1000 words. Include sensory detail, discovery, conflict, vulnerability, and risk. Add a title that pops.

Writer Vivian Gornick states, "What happened to the writer is not what matters; what matters is the large sense that the writer is able to make of what happened."

Write a 500- to 1000-word micro-memoir. Choose a defining moment and put pen to paper on the next two pages.

weekly tranquility tools

○ PLAN WEEK'S MITS　　○ SOAK IN THE TUB　　○ DIGITAL DAY OFF　　○ CLEAR CLUTTER
○ PEN A LOVE NOTE　　○ ARTIST DATE　　○ GREEN JUICE　　○ BUY OR PICK FRESH FLOWERS

my micro-memoir

monthly planner

MONTH: _____   **INTENTION:** _____

SUNDAY	MONDAY	TUESDAY	WEDNESDAY	THURSDAY	FRIDAY	SATURDAY

monthly tranquility tools and practices

- ○ CRAFT MONTH'S DREAMS
- ○ REVIEW BUDGET
- ○ WEEK 1
- ○ CREATE SOMETHING
- ○ READ TWO BOOKS
- ○ WEEK 2
- ○ VOLUNTEER
- ○ MANI/PEDI
- ○ WEEK 3
- ○ ENTERTAIN
- ○ MASSAGE
- ○ WEEK 4

month's dreams

month's review

moon phases

Notice your connection to the moon's cycles in these four phases: new, waxing, full, waning. Consider the prompts below as a way to tie into your Month's Dreams and provide space for monthly reflection.

new moon

A TIME FOR SETTING INTENTIONS.
I WANT...

waxing moon

A TIME FOR ACTION.
I WILL...

full moon

A TIME FOR HARVEST AND CLOSURE.
I RELEASE...

waning moon

A TIME FOR SOFTENING.
I FEEL...

daily checklist

TRACK YOUR INCORPORATION OF THE DAILY TRANQUILITY TOOLS.

1
- ○ MORNING ROUTINE
- ○ DAILY DRESS-UP
- ○ MINDFUL MOVEMENT
- ○ EAT YOUR VEGGIES
- ○ JOURNAL
- ○ GOAL REVIEW
- ○ GRATITUDE
- ○ EVENING ROUTINE
- ○ _____

2
- ○ MORNING ROUTINE
- ○ DAILY DRESS-UP
- ○ MINDFUL MOVEMENT
- ○ EAT YOUR VEGGIES
- ○ JOURNAL
- ○ GOAL REVIEW
- ○ GRATITUDE
- ○ EVENING ROUTINE
- ○ _____

3
- ○ MORNING ROUTINE
- ○ DAILY DRESS-UP
- ○ MINDFUL MOVEMENT
- ○ EAT YOUR VEGGIES
- ○ JOURNAL
- ○ GOAL REVIEW
- ○ GRATITUDE
- ○ EVENING ROUTINE
- ○ _____

4
- ○ MORNING ROUTINE
- ○ DAILY DRESS-UP
- ○ MINDFUL MOVEMENT
- ○ EAT YOUR VEGGIES
- ○ JOURNAL
- ○ GOAL REVIEW
- ○ GRATITUDE
- ○ EVENING ROUTINE
- ○ _____

5
- ○ MORNING ROUTINE
- ○ DAILY DRESS-UP
- ○ MINDFUL MOVEMENT
- ○ EAT YOUR VEGGIES
- ○ JOURNAL
- ○ GOAL REVIEW
- ○ GRATITUDE
- ○ EVENING ROUTINE
- ○ _____

6
- ○ MORNING ROUTINE
- ○ DAILY DRESS-UP
- ○ MINDFUL MOVEMENT
- ○ EAT YOUR VEGGIES
- ○ JOURNAL
- ○ GOAL REVIEW
- ○ GRATITUDE
- ○ EVENING ROUTINE
- ○ _____

7
- ○ MORNING ROUTINE
- ○ DAILY DRESS-UP
- ○ MINDFUL MOVEMENT
- ○ EAT YOUR VEGGIES
- ○ JOURNAL
- ○ GOAL REVIEW
- ○ GRATITUDE
- ○ EVENING ROUTINE
- ○ _____

8
- ○ MORNING ROUTINE
- ○ DAILY DRESS-UP
- ○ MINDFUL MOVEMENT
- ○ EAT YOUR VEGGIES
- ○ JOURNAL
- ○ GOAL REVIEW
- ○ GRATITUDE
- ○ EVENING ROUTINE
- ○ _____

9
- ○ MORNING ROUTINE
- ○ DAILY DRESS-UP
- ○ MINDFUL MOVEMENT
- ○ EAT YOUR VEGGIES
- ○ JOURNAL
- ○ GOAL REVIEW
- ○ GRATITUDE
- ○ EVENING ROUTINE
- ○ _____

10
- ○ MORNING ROUTINE
- ○ DAILY DRESS-UP
- ○ MINDFUL MOVEMENT
- ○ EAT YOUR VEGGIES
- ○ JOURNAL
- ○ GOAL REVIEW
- ○ GRATITUDE
- ○ EVENING ROUTINE
- ○ _____

11
- ○ MORNING ROUTINE
- ○ DAILY DRESS-UP
- ○ MINDFUL MOVEMENT
- ○ EAT YOUR VEGGIES
- ○ JOURNAL
- ○ GOAL REVIEW
- ○ GRATITUDE
- ○ EVENING ROUTINE
- ○ _____

12
- ○ MORNING ROUTINE
- ○ DAILY DRESS-UP
- ○ MINDFUL MOVEMENT
- ○ EAT YOUR VEGGIES
- ○ JOURNAL
- ○ GOAL REVIEW
- ○ GRATITUDE
- ○ EVENING ROUTINE
- ○ _____

13
- ○ MORNING ROUTINE
- ○ DAILY DRESS-UP
- ○ MINDFUL MOVEMENT
- ○ EAT YOUR VEGGIES
- ○ JOURNAL
- ○ GOAL REVIEW
- ○ GRATITUDE
- ○ EVENING ROUTINE
- ○ _____

14
- ○ MORNING ROUTINE
- ○ DAILY DRESS-UP
- ○ MINDFUL MOVEMENT
- ○ EAT YOUR VEGGIES
- ○ JOURNAL
- ○ GOAL REVIEW
- ○ GRATITUDE
- ○ EVENING ROUTINE
- ○ _____

15
- ○ MORNING ROUTINE
- ○ DAILY DRESS-UP
- ○ MINDFUL MOVEMENT
- ○ EAT YOUR VEGGIES
- ○ JOURNAL
- ○ GOAL REVIEW
- ○ GRATITUDE
- ○ EVENING ROUTINE
- ○ _____

16
- ○ MORNING ROUTINE
- ○ DAILY DRESS-UP
- ○ MINDFUL MOVEMENT
- ○ EAT YOUR VEGGIES
- ○ JOURNAL
- ○ GOAL REVIEW
- ○ GRATITUDE
- ○ EVENING ROUTINE
- ○ _____

17
- ○ MORNING ROUTINE
- ○ DAILY DRESS-UP
- ○ MINDFUL MOVEMENT
- ○ EAT YOUR VEGGIES
- ○ JOURNAL
- ○ GOAL REVIEW
- ○ GRATITUDE
- ○ EVENING ROUTINE
- ○ _____

18
- ○ MORNING ROUTINE
- ○ DAILY DRESS-UP
- ○ MINDFUL MOVEMENT
- ○ EAT YOUR VEGGIES
- ○ JOURNAL
- ○ GOAL REVIEW
- ○ GRATITUDE
- ○ EVENING ROUTINE
- ○ _____

19
- ○ MORNING ROUTINE
- ○ DAILY DRESS-UP
- ○ MINDFUL MOVEMENT
- ○ EAT YOUR VEGGIES
- ○ JOURNAL
- ○ GOAL REVIEW
- ○ GRATITUDE
- ○ EVENING ROUTINE
- ○ _____

20
- ○ MORNING ROUTINE
- ○ DAILY DRESS-UP
- ○ MINDFUL MOVEMENT
- ○ EAT YOUR VEGGIES
- ○ JOURNAL
- ○ GOAL REVIEW
- ○ GRATITUDE
- ○ EVENING ROUTINE
- ○ _____

21
- ○ MORNING ROUTINE
- ○ DAILY DRESS-UP
- ○ MINDFUL MOVEMENT
- ○ EAT YOUR VEGGIES
- ○ JOURNAL
- ○ GOAL REVIEW
- ○ GRATITUDE
- ○ EVENING ROUTINE
- ○ _____

22
- ○ MORNING ROUTINE
- ○ DAILY DRESS-UP
- ○ MINDFUL MOVEMENT
- ○ EAT YOUR VEGGIES
- ○ JOURNAL
- ○ GOAL REVIEW
- ○ GRATITUDE
- ○ EVENING ROUTINE
- ○ _____

23
- ○ MORNING ROUTINE
- ○ DAILY DRESS-UP
- ○ MINDFUL MOVEMENT
- ○ EAT YOUR VEGGIES
- ○ JOURNAL
- ○ GOAL REVIEW
- ○ GRATITUDE
- ○ EVENING ROUTINE
- ○ _____

24
- ○ MORNING ROUTINE
- ○ DAILY DRESS-UP
- ○ MINDFUL MOVEMENT
- ○ EAT YOUR VEGGIES
- ○ JOURNAL
- ○ GOAL REVIEW
- ○ GRATITUDE
- ○ EVENING ROUTINE
- ○ _____

25
- ○ MORNING ROUTINE
- ○ DAILY DRESS-UP
- ○ MINDFUL MOVEMENT
- ○ EAT YOUR VEGGIES
- ○ JOURNAL
- ○ GOAL REVIEW
- ○ GRATITUDE
- ○ EVENING ROUTINE
- ○ _____

26
- ○ MORNING ROUTINE
- ○ DAILY DRESS-UP
- ○ MINDFUL MOVEMENT
- ○ EAT YOUR VEGGIES
- ○ JOURNAL
- ○ GOAL REVIEW
- ○ GRATITUDE
- ○ EVENING ROUTINE
- ○ _____

27
- ○ MORNING ROUTINE
- ○ DAILY DRESS-UP
- ○ MINDFUL MOVEMENT
- ○ EAT YOUR VEGGIES
- ○ JOURNAL
- ○ GOAL REVIEW
- ○ GRATITUDE
- ○ EVENING ROUTINE
- ○ _____

28
- ○ MORNING ROUTINE
- ○ DAILY DRESS-UP
- ○ MINDFUL MOVEMENT
- ○ EAT YOUR VEGGIES
- ○ JOURNAL
- ○ GOAL REVIEW
- ○ GRATITUDE
- ○ EVENING ROUTINE
- ○ _____

29
- ○ MORNING ROUTINE
- ○ DAILY DRESS-UP
- ○ MINDFUL MOVEMENT
- ○ EAT YOUR VEGGIES
- ○ JOURNAL
- ○ GOAL REVIEW
- ○ GRATITUDE
- ○ EVENING ROUTINE
- ○ _____

30
- ○ MORNING ROUTINE
- ○ DAILY DRESS-UP
- ○ MINDFUL MOVEMENT
- ○ EAT YOUR VEGGIES
- ○ JOURNAL
- ○ GOAL REVIEW
- ○ GRATITUDE
- ○ EVENING ROUTINE
- ○ _____

entrepreneurship

"I'VE LEARNED THAT PEOPLE WILL FORGET WHAT YOU SAID, PEOPLE WILL FORGET WHAT YOU DID, BUT PEOPLE WILL NEVER FORGET HOW YOU MADE THEM FEEL."
—MAYA ANGELOU

That Maya Angelou quote has been my guide over the past two decades of entrepreneurship. When I hosted the Tranquil Space team farewell party after selling the studio in 2017, I incorporated this quote into my speech and encouraged others to take this mantra with them. It's gold.

Growing up in Oklahoma, I never envisioned myself starting a business. Yet when I moved to DC, finding myself disenchanted with adulting and craving community, I decided to invite strangers into my living room for yoga. This was 1999, I was 26 years old. I quickly learned that I enjoyed the process of setting up a nurturing environment, connecting with clients, and seeing the studio grow.

Over the years, I added workshops in 2000, staff, retreats, and a teacher training in 2001, a clothing line in 2002, a blog in 2004, a podcast in 2005, a book and non-profit in 2006, another location in 2007, and a 4,000-square-foot flagship location complete with chandeliers and reclaimed wood in 2008. All of this was followed by more books, online programs, a two-month Tranquility Tour across North America in a vintage camper in 2013, and, in 2017, the selling of my baby to a yoga chain.

When the studio was turning 10 in 2009, I began to ponder the next decade. How did I want it to look? How did I want to feel? What was/wasn't working? Before I could do a deep dive into this, I decided to return to graduate school to pursue a master's degree in social work with the intention of adding psychotherapy into my offerings. Little did I know then that it would be a major transition for me down the road.

During this process of running multiple businesses, connecting with an online community, and going to graduate school, I struggled to find inner peace AND productivity.

While I would never claim to have found the magic potion, I definitely have tools and experience trying to juggle both over the past 20 years. From making the leap into self-employment (scary!), to signing my first commercial lease, to taking on massive debt during a recession (super scary!), to selling a business, to opening a private psychotherapy practice, I've learned a lot along the way.

Entrepreneurship is defined by Wikipedia as "a process of designing, launching and running a new business, which is often initially a small business." Although you may not be in the market to launch a new enterprise, each day you ARE launching your own personal empire. After all, you are the boss of YOU! Benefits include creating community, developing leadership skills, seeing your work change lives, creating products and services you love, and believing in what you do.

You may love or not-so-love the term "girl boss," which has become a bit of a thing since Sophia Amoruso's best-selling book of the same name, but the concept is applicable to each of us. For example, a definition I found of a girl boss on Free Dictionary is, "a confident, capable woman who pursues her own ambitions instead of working for others or otherwise settling in life." I love it!

Now, this doesn't mean you have to run off and open your own thing, however I'll bet you're already doing a little girl bossing. Do you volunteer for an organization? Do you have a side hustle? Do you have a blog, website, YouTube channel, or podcast? Do you have a social media presence? Are you passionate about a particular cause? Do you want to make sure your life and work have an impact? And on and on.

Imagine spending your days working with your strengths and passions while calling your own shots. You can be a homemaker or a 9-to-5er working for a bank and still think of your role within the house or your role within a larger organization as a business.

Businesses need systems to run efficiently, a deep commitment to doing the best work, and a focus on creating an experience—all of that can be done in our everyday lives! Simply by showing up as the best version of ourselves. Being an entrepreneur (or anyone who goes slightly against the grain) is scary and yet so rewarding. And, frankly, is a necessity.

Poet and feminist Audre Lorde speaks to this: "Next time, ask: what's the worst that will happen? Then push yourself a little further than you dare. Once you start to speak, people will yell at you. They will interrupt you, put you down and suggest it's personal. And the world won't end. And the speaking will get easier and easier. And you will find you have fallen in love with your own vision, which you may never have realized you had. And you will lose some friends and lovers, and realize you don't miss them. And new ones will find you and cherish you. And at last you'll know with surpassing certainty that only one thing is more frightening than speaking your truth. And that is not speaking."

This month, pay attention to your longings. Observe your strengths. Consider your brand (what people think of when they hear your name). Ask yourself the hard questions (what do I want, need, and feel?) daily. Take the time to connect to your inner entrepreneur—

LET YOUR LIGHT SHINE AND ENCOURAGE OTHERS TO DO THE SAME.

she deserves to be attended to with great care and compassion. Acknowledge that part of you who wants BIG things for herself and the world. Repeat this Maya Angelou quote to yourself, "Each time a woman stands up for herself, without knowing it possibly, without claiming it, she stands up for all women." Let's go get 'em!

Savvy Sources

BOOKS:
Tranquilista by Kimberly Wilson
In the Company of Women by Grace Bonney
The $100 Startup by Chris Guillebeau
The Magic of Tiny Business by Sharon Rowe
168 Hours by Laura Vanderkam
The E-Myth by Michael Gerber
She Means Business by Carrie Green

APPS:
Evernote
SimpleMind

TRANQUILITY DU JOUR PODCASTS:
#132 Hot Mommas Project
#160 Unfold Your Life Vision
#199 168 Hours
#209 Right Brain Business Plan
#211 Dreams to Reality
#306 What Most Successful People Do at Work
#314 Building Your Biz the Right-Brain Way
#343 I Know How She Does It
#396 Start Right Where You Are
#404 Transitions

notes:

WEEK 1: PRODUCTIVITY

When asked how I juggle various projects, my answer is always that I write everything down—getting it out of my head and onto paper. I carry my planner, an ideas book, and a journal with me at all times.

My most helpful tool is clarifying weekly, and sometimes daily, MITs (Most Important Tasks). Noting what must be accomplished that day/week helps put the rest of the to-dos in perspective. This is my Sunday night exercise.

I also try to break projects into smaller tasks (remember those micromovements), so instead of "launch fall collection," I write, "choose colors" and "order lab dips."

We all wear so many hats. To avoid switching them multiple times throughout the day, I set times for handling email, writing, projects, home stuff, clients, exercise, and family. That way I can be fully present with the person or task at hand.

Productivity also needs rest. One of the biggest lessons I've learned during the past 20 years of entrepreneurship is to step away from the computer, breathe, and say "yes!" to fun, even if I have more to-dos (there always are). There are few things that a hot bath, walk, or good sleep can't fix or at least offer a fresh perspective on.

To explore your own productivity, write out everything that's on your mind. Review it for action steps to add to your to-do lists. Clarify your MITs. Track your time over the next two weeks to get an average of how you're spending it. Familiar with the 80/20 rule? Also known as the Pareto Principle, it means that 80 percent of our results come from 20 percent of our actions or, another way to look at it is, 20 percent of our work drives 80 percent of our outcomes. This rule serves as a gentle nudge to cut out the non-essentials that generate little value to declutter our time and energy so that we can focus on what matters most.

List your various hats. Explore ways to wear them during time chunks (hello, Pomodoro Technique) that align with your complementary energy level such as early morning exercise or evening writing.

Create your ideal version of the week while keeping your various hats and energy levels in mind.

Be the boss of your time and energy! As Michael Gerber of *E-Myth* fame says, "Work ON your business, not just IN your business." That way the day-to-day minutia doesn't overpower the big picture.

This week list your projects, clarify your MITs, track your time, and fill out your ideal 168 hours grid on p. 33. List a few ways to bridge any gap between the two keeping energy levels in mind.

weekly tranquility tools

- ○ PLAN WEEK'S MITS
- ○ PEN A LOVE NOTE
- ○ SOAK IN THE TUB
- ○ ARTIST DATE
- ○ DIGITAL DAY OFF
- ○ GREEN JUICE
- ○ CLEAR CLUTTER
- ○ BUY OR PICK FRESH FLOWERS

WEEK 2: PERSONAL BRAND

Your personal brand is the sum total of what you do, how you do it and why you do it. Jeff Bezos, founder of Amazon, famously said, "Your brand is what people say about you when you're not in the room."

How would you describe your personal brand? Think of it as your "secret sauce." You know, that thing that makes you YOU!

Here are a few ways to help craft it, in no particular order:

1. Build a platform through your online presence. This is your own personal stage that you share with the world.
2. Highlight your unique strengths, interests, and quirks (hello, Pigs & Pugs).
3. Become an expert in your field.
4. Share your expertise through teaching, consulting, writing, and speaking.
5. Define and identify your target market and offer a product or service that will serve your tribe.
6. Get clear on what success will look like for you in 1, 5, 10 years.
7. Be consistent in your messaging and frequency.
8. Provide value and inspiration by creating tools, tips, and tutorials.
9. Create community by commenting, posting, hosting in-person and online meetups, creating a book club or movie club—anything that will bring like-hearted people together.
10. Create emotion and an experience. For example, Pigs & Pugs shares the stories of the animals who receive our micro-grants and at my former yoga studio, we served tea and cookies at the end of each class.

This week consider your own personal brand. How would you describe it? How would you like it to be described?

weekly tranquility tools

- ○ PLAN WEEK'S MITS
- ○ PEN A LOVE NOTE
- ○ SOAK IN THE TUB
- ○ ARTIST DATE
- ○ DIGITAL DAY OFF
- ○ GREEN JUICE
- ○ CLEAR CLUTTER
- ○ BUY OR PICK FRESH FLOWERS

WEEK 3: TEACHING AND CONSULTING

TEACHING

Sharing your knowledge with others and guiding them through the process is the act of teaching. For the past two decades I've been teaching events ranging from yoga classes to international retreats to intimate salons. Teaching yoga at gyms started as a side hustle for me that grew into a full-time career.

The beauty of teaching is that I've been able to take many trainings, classes, workshops, and certificate courses over the years that contribute to my knowledge and ultimately allow me to incorporate it into my special sauce.

Here's where the interplay of personal and professional mix because I'm studying subjects I love so it doesn't feel like work per se. You know, nothing like those stodgy conferences in hotel ballrooms that we have to attend for our industry. It's different when you make a conscious choice to study, learn, and share.

Think about what you could teach. English as a second language. Coach a little league team. Spinning. Making terrariums. Macramé. Knitting. Hand lettering. Sewing. Yoga. Decorating on a budget. Minimalist parenting. Pilates. Dog training. Getting published. Managing a non-profit. Finding personal style. Personal training. And on and on.

CONSULTING

Giving advice to others based on your experience and/or studies is what consulting is all about. For years I received emails from well-meaning people wanting to take me to tea to "pick my brain" (anyone else think that phrasing is creepy?). Due to lack of time and energy (I'm an introvert so sitting with a stranger rarely entices me), I grew challenged by the requests and set up my mentoring program back in the early 2000s.

I called it mentoring because consulting felt too corporate and coaching also didn't resonate. This allowed me to direct people to an offering versus just saying no. And it allowed me to feel compensated for my time and knowledge.

Now consider what you could consult on. Moving to a new country. Health coaching. Starting a business. Growing a business. Personal stylist. Building a website. Workplace culture. Nutrition. Transitioning to plant-based eating. Decorating for the holidays. Private yoga lessons. Managing a team.

This week consider what you may be interested in incorporating into your life as a teacher and/or consultant. Is there a side hustle opportunity to spread your expertise?

weekly tranquility tools

- PLAN WEEK'S MITS
- PEN A LOVE NOTE
- SOAK IN THE TUB
- ARTIST DATE
- DIGITAL DAY OFF
- GREEN JUICE
- CLEAR CLUTTER
- BUY OR PICK FRESH FLOWERS

WEEK 4: SPEAKING AND WRITING

SPEAKING

While getting up in front of an audience is not for everyone, with a few tools, you may actually enjoy it. I first began by speaking on panels about entrepreneurship, and it's a great place to start because all eyes aren't on you. When I gave a keynote at a conference or spoke at a few corporate events, I had a standard speech that I altered for the varied audiences similar to my writing noted below.

Speaking gigs are also great opportunities to establish yourself as an expert and expand your reach. Share your products or services by placing items in goody bags or create a private page on your website that's aligned with the talk and offers more resources. Although I'm often anxious beforehand, I find myself settling in and actually enjoying it. Usually!

Here are a few tips to shine: be prepared, make eye contact with the audience, your opening is everything (include a statistic, question, or story), speak slowly (I'm a fast talker so I have to consciously slloowwww it down), encourage action and/or takeaways, and end with a summary and gratitude.

What about you? Would you like to speak at meetups, conferences, community events, book clubs, or some other setting? What's your area(s) of expertise? Share that beautiful voice of yours!

WRITING

Yes, we had an entire month dedicated to this topic, but not focused around the idea of using it as a tool to build a platform, make extra money, or create community. Writing is an effective way to do all the above. For me, it started with a blog in 2004, then a book in 2006, and it continues to be an important mode of communication.

Consider topics you LOVE and feel like an expert (of sorts) in. Maybe it's blending essential oils, telling your recovery story, or offering tips on living with less. There are magazines always looking for submissions, along with websites such as *Medium* or *Huffington Post*, and even your neighborhood newsletter.

I started with a "5 Tips to Tranquility" essay in 2000 and I tweaked it for various audiences such as my college alumnae group, a DC small business center, a DC neighborhood print newsletter, my yoga studio, and I'm sure there's a few more. That piece got a lot of play, simply because I offered it for free and the sources were looking for content.

Do you have your own version of that 5 Tips piece? Today there's even more opportunity to share via social media, blogs, podcasts, and websites. How can you spread your message via speaking or writing to grow and nurture your tribe?

weekly tranquility tools

- PLAN WEEK'S MITS
- PEN A LOVE NOTE
- SOAK IN THE TUB
- ARTIST DATE
- DIGITAL DAY OFF
- GREEN JUICE
- CLEAR CLUTTER
- BUY OR PICK FRESH FLOWERS

monthly planner

MONTH: _____   INTENTION: _____

SUNDAY	MONDAY	TUESDAY	WEDNESDAY	THURSDAY	FRIDAY	SATURDAY

monthly tranquility tools and practices

- ○ CRAFT MONTH'S DREAMS
- ○ REVIEW BUDGET
- ○ WEEK 1
- ○ CREATE SOMETHING
- ○ READ TWO BOOKS
- ○ WEEK 2
- ○ VOLUNTEER
- ○ MANI/PEDI
- ○ WEEK 3
- ○ ENTERTAIN
- ○ MASSAGE
- ○ WEEK 4

month's dreams

month's review

moon phases

Notice your connection to the moon's cycles in these four phases: new, waxing, full, waning. Consider the prompts below as a way to tie into your Month's Dreams and provide space for monthly reflection.

new moon

waxing moon

A TIME FOR SETTING INTENTIONS.
I WANT...

A TIME FOR ACTION.
I WILL...

full moon

waning moon

A TIME FOR HARVEST AND CLOSURE.
I RELEASE...

A TIME FOR SOFTENING.
I FEEL...

daily checklist

TRACK YOUR INCORPORATION OF THE DAILY TRANQUILITY TOOLS.

Day 1
- ○ MORNING ROUTINE
- ○ DAILY DRESS-UP
- ○ MINDFUL MOVEMENT
- ○ EAT YOUR VEGGIES
- ○ JOURNAL
- ○ GOAL REVIEW
- ○ GRATITUDE
- ○ EVENING ROUTINE
- ○ _____

Day 2
- ○ MORNING ROUTINE
- ○ DAILY DRESS-UP
- ○ MINDFUL MOVEMENT
- ○ EAT YOUR VEGGIES
- ○ JOURNAL
- ○ GOAL REVIEW
- ○ GRATITUDE
- ○ EVENING ROUTINE
- ○ _____

Day 3
- ○ MORNING ROUTINE
- ○ DAILY DRESS-UP
- ○ MINDFUL MOVEMENT
- ○ EAT YOUR VEGGIES
- ○ JOURNAL
- ○ GOAL REVIEW
- ○ GRATITUDE
- ○ EVENING ROUTINE
- ○ _____

Day 4
- ○ MORNING ROUTINE
- ○ DAILY DRESS-UP
- ○ MINDFUL MOVEMENT
- ○ EAT YOUR VEGGIES
- ○ JOURNAL
- ○ GOAL REVIEW
- ○ GRATITUDE
- ○ EVENING ROUTINE
- ○ _____

Day 5
- ○ MORNING ROUTINE
- ○ DAILY DRESS-UP
- ○ MINDFUL MOVEMENT
- ○ EAT YOUR VEGGIES
- ○ JOURNAL
- ○ GOAL REVIEW
- ○ GRATITUDE
- ○ EVENING ROUTINE
- ○ _____

Day 6
- ○ MORNING ROUTINE
- ○ DAILY DRESS-UP
- ○ MINDFUL MOVEMENT
- ○ EAT YOUR VEGGIES
- ○ JOURNAL
- ○ GOAL REVIEW
- ○ GRATITUDE
- ○ EVENING ROUTINE
- ○ _____

Day 7
- ○ MORNING ROUTINE
- ○ DAILY DRESS-UP
- ○ MINDFUL MOVEMENT
- ○ EAT YOUR VEGGIES
- ○ JOURNAL
- ○ GOAL REVIEW
- ○ GRATITUDE
- ○ EVENING ROUTINE
- ○ _____

Day 8
- ○ MORNING ROUTINE
- ○ DAILY DRESS-UP
- ○ MINDFUL MOVEMENT
- ○ EAT YOUR VEGGIES
- ○ JOURNAL
- ○ GOAL REVIEW
- ○ GRATITUDE
- ○ EVENING ROUTINE
- ○ _____

Day 9
- ○ MORNING ROUTINE
- ○ DAILY DRESS-UP
- ○ MINDFUL MOVEMENT
- ○ EAT YOUR VEGGIES
- ○ JOURNAL
- ○ GOAL REVIEW
- ○ GRATITUDE
- ○ EVENING ROUTINE
- ○ _____

Day 10
- ○ MORNING ROUTINE
- ○ DAILY DRESS-UP
- ○ MINDFUL MOVEMENT
- ○ EAT YOUR VEGGIES
- ○ JOURNAL
- ○ GOAL REVIEW
- ○ GRATITUDE
- ○ EVENING ROUTINE
- ○ _____

Day 11
- ○ MORNING ROUTINE
- ○ DAILY DRESS-UP
- ○ MINDFUL MOVEMENT
- ○ EAT YOUR VEGGIES
- ○ JOURNAL
- ○ GOAL REVIEW
- ○ GRATITUDE
- ○ EVENING ROUTINE
- ○ _____

Day 12
- ○ MORNING ROUTINE
- ○ DAILY DRESS-UP
- ○ MINDFUL MOVEMENT
- ○ EAT YOUR VEGGIES
- ○ JOURNAL
- ○ GOAL REVIEW
- ○ GRATITUDE
- ○ EVENING ROUTINE
- ○ _____

Day 13
- ○ MORNING ROUTINE
- ○ DAILY DRESS-UP
- ○ MINDFUL MOVEMENT
- ○ EAT YOUR VEGGIES
- ○ JOURNAL
- ○ GOAL REVIEW
- ○ GRATITUDE
- ○ EVENING ROUTINE
- ○ _____

Day 14
- ○ MORNING ROUTINE
- ○ DAILY DRESS-UP
- ○ MINDFUL MOVEMENT
- ○ EAT YOUR VEGGIES
- ○ JOURNAL
- ○ GOAL REVIEW
- ○ GRATITUDE
- ○ EVENING ROUTINE
- ○ _____

Day 15
- ○ MORNING ROUTINE
- ○ DAILY DRESS-UP
- ○ MINDFUL MOVEMENT
- ○ EAT YOUR VEGGIES
- ○ JOURNAL
- ○ GOAL REVIEW
- ○ GRATITUDE
- ○ EVENING ROUTINE
- ○ _____

Day 16
- ○ MORNING ROUTINE
- ○ DAILY DRESS-UP
- ○ MINDFUL MOVEMENT
- ○ EAT YOUR VEGGIES
- ○ JOURNAL
- ○ GOAL REVIEW
- ○ GRATITUDE
- ○ EVENING ROUTINE
- ○ _____

Day 17
- ○ MORNING ROUTINE
- ○ DAILY DRESS-UP
- ○ MINDFUL MOVEMENT
- ○ EAT YOUR VEGGIES
- ○ JOURNAL
- ○ GOAL REVIEW
- ○ GRATITUDE
- ○ EVENING ROUTINE
- ○ _____

Day 18
- ○ MORNING ROUTINE
- ○ DAILY DRESS-UP
- ○ MINDFUL MOVEMENT
- ○ EAT YOUR VEGGIES
- ○ JOURNAL
- ○ GOAL REVIEW
- ○ GRATITUDE
- ○ EVENING ROUTINE
- ○ _____

Day 19
- ○ MORNING ROUTINE
- ○ DAILY DRESS-UP
- ○ MINDFUL MOVEMENT
- ○ EAT YOUR VEGGIES
- ○ JOURNAL
- ○ GOAL REVIEW
- ○ GRATITUDE
- ○ EVENING ROUTINE
- ○ _____

Day 20
- ○ MORNING ROUTINE
- ○ DAILY DRESS-UP
- ○ MINDFUL MOVEMENT
- ○ EAT YOUR VEGGIES
- ○ JOURNAL
- ○ GOAL REVIEW
- ○ GRATITUDE
- ○ EVENING ROUTINE
- ○ _____

Day 21
- ○ MORNING ROUTINE
- ○ DAILY DRESS-UP
- ○ MINDFUL MOVEMENT
- ○ EAT YOUR VEGGIES
- ○ JOURNAL
- ○ GOAL REVIEW
- ○ GRATITUDE
- ○ EVENING ROUTINE
- ○ _____

Day 22
- ○ MORNING ROUTINE
- ○ DAILY DRESS-UP
- ○ MINDFUL MOVEMENT
- ○ EAT YOUR VEGGIES
- ○ JOURNAL
- ○ GOAL REVIEW
- ○ GRATITUDE
- ○ EVENING ROUTINE
- ○ _____

Day 23
- ○ MORNING ROUTINE
- ○ DAILY DRESS-UP
- ○ MINDFUL MOVEMENT
- ○ EAT YOUR VEGGIES
- ○ JOURNAL
- ○ GOAL REVIEW
- ○ GRATITUDE
- ○ EVENING ROUTINE
- ○ _____

Day 24
- ○ MORNING ROUTINE
- ○ DAILY DRESS-UP
- ○ MINDFUL MOVEMENT
- ○ EAT YOUR VEGGIES
- ○ JOURNAL
- ○ GOAL REVIEW
- ○ GRATITUDE
- ○ EVENING ROUTINE
- ○ _____

Day 25
- ○ MORNING ROUTINE
- ○ DAILY DRESS-UP
- ○ MINDFUL MOVEMENT
- ○ EAT YOUR VEGGIES
- ○ JOURNAL
- ○ GOAL REVIEW
- ○ GRATITUDE
- ○ EVENING ROUTINE
- ○ _____

Day 26
- ○ MORNING ROUTINE
- ○ DAILY DRESS-UP
- ○ MINDFUL MOVEMENT
- ○ EAT YOUR VEGGIES
- ○ JOURNAL
- ○ GOAL REVIEW
- ○ GRATITUDE
- ○ EVENING ROUTINE
- ○ _____

Day 27
- ○ MORNING ROUTINE
- ○ DAILY DRESS-UP
- ○ MINDFUL MOVEMENT
- ○ EAT YOUR VEGGIES
- ○ JOURNAL
- ○ GOAL REVIEW
- ○ GRATITUDE
- ○ EVENING ROUTINE
- ○ _____

Day 28
- ○ MORNING ROUTINE
- ○ DAILY DRESS-UP
- ○ MINDFUL MOVEMENT
- ○ EAT YOUR VEGGIES
- ○ JOURNAL
- ○ GOAL REVIEW
- ○ GRATITUDE
- ○ EVENING ROUTINE
- ○ _____

Day 29
- ○ MORNING ROUTINE
- ○ DAILY DRESS-UP
- ○ MINDFUL MOVEMENT
- ○ EAT YOUR VEGGIES
- ○ JOURNAL
- ○ GOAL REVIEW
- ○ GRATITUDE
- ○ EVENING ROUTINE
- ○ _____

Day 30
- ○ MORNING ROUTINE
- ○ DAILY DRESS-UP
- ○ MINDFUL MOVEMENT
- ○ EAT YOUR VEGGIES
- ○ JOURNAL
- ○ GOAL REVIEW
- ○ GRATITUDE
- ○ EVENING ROUTINE
- ○ _____

meaning

"THE PURPOSE OF LIFE IS NOT TO BE HAPPY. IT IS TO BE USEFUL, TO BE HONORABLE, TO BE COMPASSIONATE, TO HAVE IT MAKE SOME DIFFERENCE IN THAT YOU HAVE LIVED AND LIVED WELL." —RALPH WALDO EMERSON

When choosing the 12 topics for Year of Tranquility, I landed upon meaning as the ideal final module for our work together this year. Why? Because it's an important, often overlooked concept in our day-to-day lives that can serve as a roadmap and help us tie a bow around this year.

According to a 2015 study by researchers Frank Martela and Michael Steger, the meaning of life means coherence, purpose, and significance. They define coherence as "a sense of comprehensibility and one's life making sense." According to the authors, purpose is "a sense of core goals, aims, and direction in life." Significance is "a sense of life's inherent value and having a life worth living."

They note that understanding meaning isn't asking the philosophical question "What's the meaning of life?," but rather "looking at the subjective experiences of human beings and asks what makes them experience meaningfulness in their lives." For example, "Where's the meaning in my life?"

We'll look at the meaning IN life (personal) versus the meaning OF life (philosophical) this month through various practices and reflections. Again, I believe this ties in perfectly with *Year of Tranquility*'s final module and I hope you do, too!

Throughout my adult life, I've sought meaning in creating community and offering products or services that help others experience meaning. For example, seeing a yoga student grow confidently on the mat, a therapy client begin to set boundaries, or a retreat participant have an aha has been a motivating factor.

Also, I've found that two of my biggest losses—losing Gramma and my beloved pug Louis—forced me to pause and do deeper reflection that ultimately led to me turning over daily studio operations and then to even stop teaching weekly yoga classes.

Without these two big existential knockdowns, I wouldn't have made these changes. At least not at that time. I didn't feel like I could until these two losses forced me into a mindset shift.

One important thing I've come to learn over the years is that what we do does not create the meaning, but rather it's the meaning we assign to what we do. Similar to the therapeutic phrase "the story I'm telling myself is . . ."

For example, when we assign meaning to an email that we don't necessarily know to be true such as, "Wow, she must be really upset with me," we're telling ourselves a story about a situation. Considering our thoughts are not reality (shocking, I know!), these stories can lead us down interesting and sometimes challenging rabbit holes.

The difference in the meaning we assign to experiences is illustrated in the story about two bricklayers who are asked what they're doing.

INFUSE
THE DAY WITH SIMPLE DELIGHTS AND SWEET MOMENTS.

One replies with something along the lines of, "stacking bricks on top of each other" and the other replies with, "creating a cathedral."

Our ability to see the bigger picture—you know, to take that bird's eye view—offers us the chance to recognize how we're contributing to making the world a better place. And you do that every single day in various ways.

The founder of positive psychology, Martin Seligman, wrote, "For a person to be truly happy and live a meaningful life, that person must recognize their personal strengths and use these strengths for the greater good." This month we'll ask questions, explore meaning-making practices, learn about transitions, and even create a life purpose statement. Meaning is found within and lived without by being of service and leaving a legacy.

Savvy Sources

BOOKS:
The Power of Meaning by Emily Esfahani Smith
Man's Search for Meaning by Viktor Frankl
Joyful by Ingrid Fetell Lee
Transitions by William Bridges
Finding Meaning in the Second Half of Life by James Hollis
The Meandering River of Unfathomable Joy by Christine Mason Miller
Flow by Mihaly Csikszentmihaly

APPS:
Gratitude 365
Life Purpose

TRANQUILITY DU JOUR PODCASTS:
#116 Spiritual Activism
#328 Life Purpose Bootcamp
#336 Women Entrepreneur Revolution
#359 Artistic Activism
#428 Transitions

1
WEEK 1: REFLECTION

As we come to the final few weeks of our program, this idea of meaning feels so pertinent. What is it that brings YOU meaning?

This week spend time in quiet reflection. Notice what comes up. There's no right or wrong here, just notice. Grab a cup of tea, a pen, and ponder these questions.

1. What has brought you to this place in your journey?
2. What's one thing you could do today that your future self would thank you for?
3. Think of what would be unlived if your life ended today.
4. How will you leave a legacy?
5. What's on your bucket list?
6. What makes you come alive?

weekly tranquility tools

- ○ PLAN WEEK'S MITS
- ○ PEN A LOVE NOTE
- ○ SOAK IN THE TUB
- ○ ARTIST DATE
- ○ DIGITAL DAY OFF
- ○ GREEN JUICE
- ○ CLEAR CLUTTER
- ○ BUY OR PICK FRESH FLOWERS

WEEK 2: MAKING MEANING

As we spend time exploring meaning in our own lives, it can be helpful to reflect on various ways to connect to it. Below you'll find a smattering of ways to infuse more meaning into every day.

- Ponder the fleeting nature of life.
- Do activities that make you happy. What did you love as a child?
- Be in nature; get outside daily.
- Challenge yourself by trying something different: a new language, a new form of movement, or a new genre of music, book, or film.
- Connect with others, make tea dates, host gatherings, reach out.
- Celebrate those small, everyday wins that deserve acknowledgement.
- Express gratitude.
- Show compassion toward self and others. As Plato said, "Be kind for everyone is fighting a hard battle."
- Give back. Volunteer, donate, host a chariTea (how-to at kimberlywilson.com/treasures).
- Get into the flow, which is that optimal state of consciousness where you feel and perform your best.
- Create community at work, school, biz, place of worship, neighborhood.
- Pay close attention to your senses.
- Set goals and track them.

weekly tranquility tools

- PLAN WEEK'S MITS
- PEN A LOVE NOTE
- SOAK IN THE TUB
- ARTIST DATE
- DIGITAL DAY OFF
- GREEN JUICE
- CLEAR CLUTTER
- BUY OR PICK FRESH FLOWERS

WEEK 3: 4 PILLARS OF MEANING

Pulling from positive psychology and philosophy, Emily Esfahani Smith penned *The Power of Meaning: Finding Fulfillment in a World Obsessed with Happiness*. In the book and in her TED Talk, she lays out the four pillars of meaning. Let's look at these to consider how we, too, can implement them into our everyday lives.

BELONGING

As social creatures, we have a deep need to be seen, valued, and understood by our family and friends. She describes a meaningful relationship as "where you really feel like you matter to others and are valued by them, and where you in turn treat others like they matter and are valued." By focusing on others, we are able to build the pillar of belonging through reaching out, being present, and creating small moments of intimacy. This can be done with close relationships and even strangers. Ever had those deep conversations with someone you randomly sat next to on a train?

PURPOSE

The author writes that although living with purpose may make us happier, it's really about using our strengths and talents to make the world a better place. She notes that our calling is different from purpose and that while we may not find our calling, we can still find purpose by seeing what we do as a way to help others, focusing on the bigger picture, and, ultimately, leaving a legacy. Remember the story of the bricklayer—one is laying bricks, one is building a cathedral.

STORYTELLING

Stories help us better understand who we are and how we got to be who we are. They are our very own personal myths. Reflecting on how we came to be ourselves and consciously creating our future story can find meaning. The author notes that as the writers of our stories, we can change the way we're telling them by editing and reinterpreting them. This can lead to feeling more in control and to recognize meaning that came out of hard experiences. Reflecting on those big life moments such as a late night phone call or the death of a loved one to note how they shaped us contributes to a sense of meaning.

TRANSCENDENCE

This is a mental state of deep focus and engagement where we lose our sense of self and feel deeply connected to a bigger picture. Psychologists call this "flow" and Mihaly Csikszentmihalyi has written extensively about this concept. It may be found in a ballet performance, a sporting event, planting tomato seeds in the garden, meditation, or anything in between. In these moments our daily concerns may seem small because we're so absorbed in the world that lies beyond ourselves.

This week consider the idea of belonging, purpose, storytelling, and transcendence. Can you reach out to someone in a meaningful way, consider ways to use your strengths to benefit others, reframe your story to see the meaning, and/or lose yourself in a transcendent experience?

weekly tranquility tools

- PLAN WEEK'S MITS
- PEN A LOVE NOTE
- SOAK IN THE TUB
- ARTIST DATE
- DIGITAL DAY OFF
- GREEN JUICE
- CLEAR CLUTTER
- BUY OR PICK FRESH FLOWERS

WEEK 4: TRANSITIONS AND LIFE PURPOSE

In the book *Transitions*, author William Bridges describes change as situational and transition as psychological. He goes on, "Changes are driven to reach a goal, but transitions start with letting go of what no longer fits or is adequate to the life stage you are in. It is internal—something you've believed or assumed, some way you've always been or seen yourself, some outlook on the world or attitude toward others." Is there a role (e.g., boss, girlfriend, yoga teacher), identity (e.g., our values and beliefs), or action (e.g., putting others first) that no longer resonates or serves you?

He also describes the three parts of transition as: ending, the neutral zone, a new beginning. We have to thoroughly move through the neutral zone (a time of confusion and distress) before we can start the new beginning phase. Although endings such as moving out of your home, leaving a relationship, or quitting a job may feel traumatic in the moment, Bridges claims that endings are the first, not the last, act of our life play. They open us up to what's next.

A positive mindset helps us through transition by being proactive and engaged versus numbing out and avoiding. Keeping a routine can also contribute to feeling more in control when so much around us is in flux. And, of course, looking for meaning in the transition is another way to move through it with more ease.

According to positive psychology, life purpose is a Venn diagram of what you love, what you do, how you shine, and your experiences.

A life purpose statement contains three pieces synthesized into one to two sentences that serve as a guidepost. Start with a list of the many ways that you shine. Next, note how you express these skills and abilities. Then, list a variety of passions and dreams. Finally, combine the three into a statement. For example, "My purpose is to use my creativity to bring beauty into the world to support and inspire others."

weekly tranquility tools

○ PLAN WEEK'S MITS
○ PEN A LOVE NOTE
○ SOAK IN THE TUB
○ ARTIST DATE
○ DIGITAL DAY OFF
○ GREEN JUICE
○ CLEAR CLUTTER
○ BUY OR PICK FRESH FLOWERS

seasonal life review

DATE: _____

SEASONALLY REFLECT ON AREAS OF YOUR LIFE. RATE EACH ONE
WITH YOUR LEVEL OF SATISFACTION 10 = BLISS, 5 = SO-SO, 0 = BOO.

Here are some additional areas to consider: social life, romance, family, education, health, fitness, meaning, activism. Next, take a moment to note the areas that ranked low and create three action steps to increase your tranquility in these areas. Be gentle. Plant seeds. Watch dreams take root.

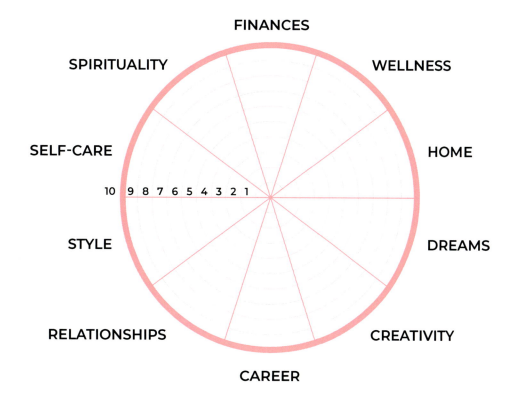

ACTION STEPS TO INCREASE AREAS THAT ARE LOWER THAN I'D LIKE:

seasonal checklist

- ○ WHEEL OF LIFE
- ○ DEEP CLEAN
- ○ PRACTICE ESSENTIALISM
- ○ TRY SOMETHING NEW
- ○ BED DAY
- ○ REARRANGE
- ○ GET CULTURED
- ○ TEND YOUR GARDEN
- ○ _____

MAY ALL BEINGS EVERYWHERE BE HAPPY AND FREE.

tying a bow

"FOR LAST YEAR'S WORDS BELONG TO LAST YEAR'S LANGUAGE. AND NEXT YEAR'S WORDS AWAIT ANOTHER VOICE. AND TO MAKE AN END IS TO MAKE A BEGINNING."
—T.S. ELIOT

Our journey together began with the exploration of dreams nearly one year ago. Since then we've touched on a variety of topics and practices that build on one other and contribute to a life lived with intention and ease.

As reminded throughout, there was no right or wrong way to do this program. However you've shown up for the adventure, you did it perfectly and deserve a gold star simply by being here. The material is here for you to dive back into at any time. Start fresh with dreams or begin with a favorite module and review the practices at your leisure.

Keep these lessons close to your heart as you tie a bow around this year and prepare for a brand new one. Remember those micromovements, that necessary dose of self-compassion, your expression of signature style and beauty, the various elements of self-care and wellness, those mindfulness and yoga practices, the awareness of minimalism, that you ARE a writer and entrepreneur, to express your creativity, and to watch for ways to connect with meaning.

It's been an absolute honor to host you through this journey. Please know this isn't the end; it's the beginning of what's to come. Let your light shine. Get out there and make a difference. Reach out and let me know how *Year of Tranquility* has affected you, I'd love to hear. I'm rooting for you and believe in you!

year's review

a letter to my future self

ATTACH AN ENVELOPE WITH YOUR LETTER FROM P. 57 TO REVIEW AT YEAR'S END.

inspiration pages

USE THESE PAGES TO DOODLE, LIST, COLLAGE, OR WRITE WHAT'S INSPIRING YOU.

love note

Thank you for your gracious support of this book. These *Year of Tranquility tools were crafted with lots of love, and I hope they've been a source of inspiration for designing your year with intention.*

Your purchase helps support petite female-owned businesses, pig sanctuaries and pug rescues, and the planting of 500 trees. What we do has a compassionate ripple effect, so thank you again!

Let's grab a virtual cuppa tea and connect via Love Notes, the blog, podcasts, and online courses. Or indulge in real life on a retreat or in a salon offering. I hope our paths will cross online, in person, or in spirit this year.

I'm honored to be alongside you on this journey. You are beautiful.

bisous,
Kimberly

about kimberly

I'm a writer, psychotherapist in private practice, and designer of the locally-sewn, eco-friendly TranquiliT clothing line. I also serve as the president of Pigs & Pugs Project with a mission to make the lives of pigs and pugs happier. I dream of Paris and global animal welfare.

You'll often find me sipping fragrant green tea, in pink ballet slippers practicing demi-pliés and dégagés, or leading retreats around the world.

I have master's degrees in women's studies and social work, certificates in journal therapy and applied positive psychology, and am currently studying veterinary social work. My work has been featured in *US News & World Report*, *Washingtonian*, *Fast Company*, and *Bella Grace*.

I live in a petite pink palace in Washington, DC, with a rescue kitty, three rescue pugs, and my partner Tim. Indulge in tranquilosophy via my blog and podcast, *Tranquility du Jour*, and online courses.

#YEAROFTRANQUILITY

KIMBERLYWILSON.COM

 @TRANQUILITYDUJOUR

 @TRANQUILITYDUJOUR

 @TRANQUILITYDUJOUR

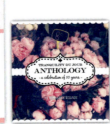

Made in the USA
Lexington, KY
01 February 2019